What are these strawberries doing on my nipples?...

...I need them for the fruit salad!

A Guide To Sub-Duvet Life
As We Know It

VANESSA FELTZ

Illustrations by Kathryn Lamb

LITTLE, BROWN AND COMPANY

A Little, Brown book

First published in Great Britain by
Little, Brown and Company in 1994

A CIP catalogue record for this book
is available from the British Library.

Typeset by Solidus (Bristol) Limited
Printed and bound in Great Britain by
Clays Ltd, St Ives plc

ISBN 0 316 91050 3

Little, Brown and Company (UK) Limited
Brettenham House
Lancaster Place
London WC2E 7EN

Dedication

For my darling husband Michael
– soul-mate, sole mate, whole mate, hot date --
with love and gratitude for your love and latitude.
For my exquisite daughters Allegra Sybilla and Saskia Clemency,
who aren't old enough to read this yet,
with kisses and cuddles from Mummy.

Contents

🍓 Contents

Contents 🍓

Acknowledgements

I wish to extend manifold thanks, exuberant hugs and flasks of chicken soup to literary diva Judith Chilcote without whom strawberries would never have met nipples and Linda Kelsey, legendary editor of SHE magazine, without whom I would have continued to blush unseen.

Is 3 Minutes In The Commercial Break of LA Law Normal?

1

How Often Is Everyone Else Doing It?

Seconds after the compulsory birds and bees talk, my mother chewed daintily on a Rich Tea and said: 'Of course, your Father and I only did it twice. Once for you, and once for your sister, Julia.'

I was six. I believed her. Now I'm thirty-two and a quarter. I still believe her. After all, parents aren't supposed to mesh genitals. It takes years of therapy at £40 per complex before we can comfortably contemplate Mum in thigh-high PVC, bringing the rolling pin down smartly on Dad's bristly bottie. Parents are for procreating us, not for sending Polaroids of one another's erectile tissue recorded delivery to 'Readers' Wives'.

So you'll agree, a twice in a lifetime delve beneath the winceyette is quite animal enough for Ma and Pa, thank you very much. But what about us? We ex-*Cosmo* girls of the post-permissive pill-popping generation? Is our fornicating frequency up to par? Are we sexual bran-eaters, reassuringly regular in our carnal habits? Or are we far more likely to get our legs waxed than over? Let's face it, sussing DNA is a mere bagatelle. The unchallenged hot contender for Greatest Unsolved Mystery Of Our Time continues to make mincemeat of our equilibrium. How often, goddammit, is everyone else doing it?

From where I'm Ladyshaving, sex is a bit like pubic hair really. Pubically speaking, no woman ever knows if she's normal. One innocent adolescent evening of blackhead evacuation, you spy a solitary brunette tuft wafting milli-metres outside your regulation school knicker-leg. You panic; naturally, you do. For all you know, you'll end up a centrefold in *National Geographic*. Never in the history of mainstream women's magazines has a single pube been known to erupt from the eternal equilateral triangle of bikinidom.

You consider the options.

1 Swallow your Clearasil and die a lingering death, pores unblocked.
2 Run away and be awfully nice to Gerry Cottle.
3 Audition for a starring role in 'Prisoner of Cell Block H'? Which to choose? How the hell should you know? You're trapped in the worst 'Even Your Best Friend Wouldn't Tell You' situation.
Desperately, you try:
4 Hanging around the changing room at Richard Shops hoping to sneak comparative peaks without buying a reduced pink polyester camisole at the 'bargain' price of £14.99.

What you don't realise is that Josephine Public is contort-ing herself into human origami to make absolutely totally completely super-certain you don't catch the thatch on her snatch. Why? Because she also plays hostess to a few sub-gusset danglers. Women will cheerfully display warts, love-bites, tattoos, stretch-marks, cellulite and even – when we hit rock bottom – piles. What we will NOT risk is coming out of the pubic closet. Why not? In case some other woman glimpses our unplucked pudenda, screams, 'Aargh!

Yikes! Look everyone, Planet of the Apes!' and has to be helicoptered to casualty, that's why not.

All we want, when the pubic/sexual french fries are down, is to be a good average. But it's hellish aspiring to the happy medium when no-one will tell you what the heck it is. To tell the truth, ever since I saw Claire Rayner rolling a condom on a cucumber, I've been bewildered. Did you, for example, know how to react when Ralph Halpern's 'Five Times A Night' frolics throbbed at you from the tabloids? I was flummoxed. Should I go for:

1 Gobsmacked envious admiration? 'Cor! More power to your dip-stick! Surprised it hasn't worn out Ralphie-Boy!'
2 Cool nonchalance? 'Five? Naturally. Doesn't everyone?'
3 Or pitying disdain? 'Only five? Poor chap. Book your prostate in for an MOT'

Luckily for you, I write about sex for a living. It may not do much for the mortgage, but at least it gives me the right to say: 'Do you enjoy having your testicles tickled?' to total strangers. It's extraordinary. I only had to sit on Granada TV's settee next to Richard and Judy once, with the word 'sexpert' flashing across my cleavage, and suddenly everyone, from my daughter's headmistress to the kosher butcher, formed a queue to spill their bedroom beans. 'Hang on a mo!' I yelled. 'Before we progress to vacuum cleaner attachments, knicker-sniffing and weeing all over each other, could we just get Back to Basics. How often do you do it?'

Kinsey, Shere Hite and the gang may not admit it, but I will. Ask the woman in the sheets about her boudoir performance, and she lies her thighs off. Not little white ones either. Great big commandment-smashing black ones. It's like doing the Cosmo Quiz.

Question 3.
How many orgasms have you notched up in 24 hours?
a 0–1
b 2–4
c 5–10.

Do we put a)? No way, bidet. If you score zilcho points, you're forced to read the humiliating 'Face It: You're A Frigid Failure' paragraph at the bottom. Do we put c)? Fat chance. Who can cope with 'Clamp Your Clit: You're A Nympho'?

Instead, we go for safe suburban b) 'Congrats! Brilliant Big O's, Babe!' Are we fibbing? Sure we are. Four orgasms in one day? Not since we discovered the spin cycle on the washer/dryer (more of that later).

The moral

Sexual revelations are always a heady mixture of fantasy, fiction and plain old shagging dog stories. Fortunately, *in vino* – or in most cases, two G & Ts and a Diet Tango and Malibu – *veritas*. Get your pals drunk as schmucks and the clitty gritty has a way of bubbling, belch-like and unbidden, to the surface. The truth, when it happens, is always frighteningly bizarre. A doctor friend of mine was asked, in his misspent youth, to conduct a bowel movement survey. Jobbies were his job, poor chap. Daily, he trudged round the hospital with clipboard and Parker, asking every patient the identical question: 'How often do you open your bowels?' Now, here's where sex and defecation part company. People don't fib about pooh-pooh. We don't bullshit, because we don't give a shit about shit. There are no macho points for multiple sittings. So, those patients cut the crap and dished out the truth. 'Take a dump, Doc? Just like everyone else, really. Eight times a day.' Or alternatively, 'Do a number 2? I'm pretty average, Doc. Once a fortnight, you could set your watch by me.' Were they abnormal? They didn't think so.

Thereby hangs a moral: normal, schnormal! If once a year, with a mouthful of mince-pies and mistletoe up your orifice takes the edge off your appetites – terrif. If the last Friday in the month suffices – fine. If you can't sleep without tube-emptying, and that includes siestas – great. And if you genuinely can't function without nookie in the morning, nookie in the evening, nookie at suppertime, send me your fax number.

I know what you're thinking, 'Morals be stuffed! I STILL want to know how often everyone else is doing it?' OK. Keep your hair on. I'll tell you all I know. Twice a week. There it is, in uncompromising black and white. Now do you feel better … or worse? Once the first unthrottled thrill wears off, Mr and Mrs Monogamy (or Partner and Partner Monogamy, lest I alienate the uncertified) partake of one another's fruits no more than twice in seven days. Seriously speaking, I'm talking one weary mid-week dip and a slightly more prolonged weekend pronging. We manage more on holiday. More when we're poorer. And more when the video's on the blink. We manage less at that time of the month. Some call it 'the curse'. I call it 'the blessing'. The perfect cry off, simpler than a headache – you don't have to swig two Panadol and lie in a darkened room with a wet flannel on your head – and I've never yet met a man who dared say 'Prove it!'

NON-MENSTRUAL
REASONS FOR
DOING IT LESS

- hot weather
- cold weather
- too little money
- too much money
- working too hard
- not working hard
  enough
- misery
- happiness
- being pre-menstrual
- worrying about
  being
  pre/post-menstrual
- cooking for the
  freezer
- curbing your
  cuticles
- because he waits till
  he's IN bed to take
  his socks off
- because he really
  wants to, and you
  bloody well wish
  you'd married that
  charming
  accountant with the
  Morris Marina.

NON-MENSTRUAL
REASONS FOR
DOING IT MORE

- pass

Now you know how often everybody else is doing it and you still feel lousy. You know WHAT average is, but you'll never know WHO it is. You scraped Maths O level. You've a pretty strong grasp of the situation. You can't take comfort from twice a week because some couples are shredding the duvet, managing much, much more, so you still can't be sure if you're measuring up. But you CAN take heart from this. They're probably not enjoying it.

8

2

How Much Is Everyone Else Enjoying It?

Don't think I don't know why you flicked to a chapter called 'How Much Is Everyone Else Enjoying It?' Confess. You were hoping for frigidity, frustration and a brace of blue balls at the very least. Relax, Reader, you came to the right place. There must be millions of long-term monogamous couples (henceforth known as long-monogs) being multiply-orgasmic right through News at Ten, but you've read enough about them in *Men Only*. (Don't ask HOW I know you read it. I just know, OK.) There are probably frenzied, yet tantalisingly tender copulators in Neasden, Abergavenny, historic Warwick and even parts of Macclesfield currently scooping Häagen-Dazs into one another's secretions and yelling: 'Yes! Yes! Yes!', but I've never met one. There may well be Sharon Stone clones, flashing their fissures in Solihull, but no-one I know knows any. Statistically speaking there have to be librarians and quantity surveyors, wantonly staining the Axminster, as they dribble tinned pineapple chunks all over each other, à la Kim and Mick in *9½ Weeks*, buttocks rippling in the gas-effect-log-fire-light. Maybe, but not in NW11.

Sod the sexperts. It's truth time. Linking labia with the same old member week in (or should I say weak in) week out, lacks a certain something on the pizzazz front. Nothing personal, but twelve years down the line, his winkle would have to play 'Lara's Theme', light up, or at least have a Georgian hallmark to get us really interested. Most sex has very little to do with enjoyment. Despite the hype, that's not what we do it for. Looked at logically, long-term sex is very like breakfast. When was the last time you got majorly excited about half a bowl of Coco Pops and a mug of instant? Not since you found the free Flintstones sticker in the packet, right? If your spouse (or common-law concubine, I'm not fussy) looked up from Nigel Dempster and said: 'Are you enjoying your breakfast, dear?' you'd be quite justified in bashing him over the head with a Kellogg's Pop-Tart. Why? Because gulping down your daily bread has a low-to-zilcho fun factor. You wouldn't go without because breakfast is what you do in the mornings. If you didn't you'd be starving at 10.30 and abuse your finely-honed size 14 with a handful of digestives and a bakewell tart. Granted, if you jumped straight on the Bakerloo without so much as a marmalade crispbread, you might well genuinely miss breakfast. But mid-morning Muesli mourning doesn't mean you regularly throb with total body gastronomic gratification even when you do manage three shreddies.

Long-term same-partner sex never approaches the cholesterol-packed punch of a 'Full English'. It's more a 'Continental'. It's best to think of marital grapplings as a croissant. It's dry, flaky and unimaginative, but it's significantly perkier with jam on and you'd kick yourself later if you refused it. 'A croissant?' I hear you ask. 'Don't be ridiculous. What about creative cunnilingus and gushing G-spots? What about tying each other to the bed-post with old popsocks and sucking spaghetti off each other's elbows?'

What about it? I'll tell you what about it. No-one ever does it except actors, who are gay off camera and have their Calvin Kleins on under the duvet, and Stephen Norris. The rest of us pride ourselves on the few spectacular nights of genital aerobics accomplished in the first flush of lust. We were radiator-hot in those ready beddy go early days of the relationship. Remember those sweetly selfless shags? 'May I lick yours?' 'No, please, let me lick yours.' 'After you, sugar-bottom.' 'No, after you, thrilly-willy. I insist.' 'We've done it on the bathmat/chopping board/hearth rug/tool kit. How about christening the cat litter?' 'Darling, I thought you'd never ask.'

Have you maintained this level of innovative abandon? Of course you haven't. Have I? Are you kidding? Has anyone else? Wise up. Sensational sex is something you watch at your local fleapit while scraping Cornetto off your trousers. It takes scriptwriters, lighting and camera people, producers, directors, vats of panstick, nipple rouge, testicular padding, a best boy and a key grip not to mention actors specially selected to 'Give good groan'. Do real-life long-monogs ever experience celluloid-quality sex? Absolutely. It has been known to happen, on birthdays, in the back of Morris Minors and after exaggerated consumption of intoxicating liquor. It just hasn't been known to happen very often.

So how much is everyone else enjoying it? Let me put it this way: given the choice between exploring each other's crevices into the small hours, or getting a decent night's kip, wouldn't you lunge for the option that leaves longest till the alarm goes off? I know I would. In March 1994, *Good Housekeeping* magazine published the results of a nationwide survey revealing that nearly half (43 per cent) of British womanhood would rather have a wonderful meal

than make love. I was staggered, till I found the bit that said two fifths of female Brits admit to being secret eaters. Here's the route to truth. Add the secret eaters to the 43 per cent, plus the secret secret eaters who are so secret they don't tell anyone. Then tot up the anorexics, women who've just had their wisdom teeth out, vegans, Seventh Day Adventists and ladies whose husbands/paramours were hovering over them as they ticked the little survey boxes. Now you have what I'd call A CONCLUSIVE RESULT. 99.9 per cent of monogamous women would far rather have a good meal than a good feel.

OK, we've come clean, we'd rather de-flea the gerbil than get conjugal. But do fun and frolics break out when we DO finally get round to it? Frankly, it depends.

REASONS NOT TO ENJOY MARITAL SEX

- You have a cold.
- He has a cold.
- The children/dog/hamster has a cold.
- The room is cold.
- Halfway through you suddenly remember your eldest's verruca.
- Halfway through it's suddenly completely through.
- He reminds you of your father.
- You remind him of your father.
- You usually fantasise about Liam Neeson, but tonight you keep getting his nose wrong.
- His idea of 'talking dirty' is unblocked drains.
- Your idea of 'talking dirty' is too dirty to talk.
- If he doesn't hurry up, you'll miss Newsnight.

Marital sex can be ...

- A Big Mac – it's over terribly quickly and later, on the loo, you wonder whether it was such a great idea after all.

- A British Rail sandwich – soggy, bog-boring and you can't get the sodding wrapper off.
- An episode of EastEnders – deeply depressing and at the end you still can't work out who's doing what to whom.
- Pavarotti in the Park – wet and noisy with glimpses of royalty.
- Downright fab – suddenly your fitted wardrobes start doing the samba, the double-glazing quadruples, a nightingale sings in Berkley Square and sparks zoom out of your uterus.

So, of course everyone else IS enjoying it – sometimes. If they claim a 100 per cent seismic sex-life, they're talking a load of old condoms.

REASONS TO ENJOY MARITAL SEX

- You might as well, it's the only sort you've been offered.
- It's your birthday.
- You probably won't do it again till Friday week.
- It's the first time for ages no-one in the family/neighbourhood has a cold.
- He reminds you of your father.
- With your contacts out she looks like Virginia Bottomley.
- Newsnight's never been up to much since Sir Robin left.
- She's bitten the top off a Walnut Whip and stuck the rest on top of your helmet.
- An orgasm burns off twenty-seven calories and you never should have eaten that Walnut Whip.

❦ 3 ❦

Have They Found Their
G-spots? If So, Where?

To tell you the truth, I'd adore not to believe in G-spots. For years I didn't. In fact, I used to be an evangelical non-believer. 'G-spots? Bollocks!' I'd remark loudly in public places. 'Absolutely!' total strangers would reply, veritably gibbering with relief. And then, as asphyxiatingly mortgaged members of the chattering classes do, we gave a dinner party. Not the buy-in-a-butler-and-hoist-aloft-the-family-silver sort, you understand. More the bung-the-butter-dish-over-the-stain-on-the-tablecloth-would-you-prefer-pasta-or-pasta type affair. Anyway, the M & S smoked salmon mousses were swimming down a treat, which evidently put one guest in mind of things vaginal. 'G-spots. What a bore!' she said, 'Stephen's practically worn out his index finger ferreting around for mine. Eight years fumbling – and not a sausage.' Cue guffaws from Yours Truly, Yours Truly's Husb, and all Yours Truly's Chums, except one couple, let's call them Lipschitz.

Naturally, the two non-laughers stuck out like a couple of sore proverbials. Why the heck weren't they succumbing to peer pressure and taking the razz out of the Big G? 'G-spots,' we crowed contagiously. 'What a farce! No such thing! Load of cobblers! Don't you think so Lipschitzes?'

Nope. Not a titter. The Lipschitz could see nowt to chortle about. Why? Because, where we have redundant bits of internal tubing, the Lipschitz turned out have fully functioning mega-kilowat G-spots. Much to our chagrin, Their Smugnesses were none other than seasoned G-spotters. Apparently, She has Him impeccably trained to home straight in on hers from a five mile radius. Over plates of steaming spag, they flaunted their expertise and wallowed in our undisguised envy.

Les Lipschitzes have spent many a congenial half hour G-spot probing and both swear everything it says in those 'Gotcher G-spot!' books is pure, unadulterated gospel. Ping a G-spot and it shoots waves of inexorable ecstasy through every vein and sinew, right through to your nail extensions. Massage a G-spot and quadrophonic jacuzzis squirt from your vaginal walls and form a puddle on the Allied Carpet. Tickle a G-spot and the earth doesn't just move, it lambadas. Frankly, by dessert time, we wenches could scarcely sit still. What cared we for caramelised tangerines when there was a fellow sitting just a profiterole away with the fingertips to turn our insides into the Fontana de Trevi? For too long our G-spots had blushed unseen. Suddenly, here we were, breaking Hovis with Christopher Columbus-Lipschitz, yet having to keep our uncharted territories stuck in our Janet Reger's for the sake of propriety. Was I the first to break down and offer Mrs Lipschitz hard cash for a ten minute archaeological session with her husband? Maybe so. Would Mrs Lipschitz oblige and hand over her spouse's digits to facilitate my rude awakening? The selfish sow wouldn't even consider it.

Did the other 'ladies' present offer Mr Lipschitz a year's free pedicure/car valeting/tiramisu in return for locating their golden Gs? Naturally, they did. Did he start salivating and put on his rubber gloves? Of course, poor man, he's only human. Did their husbands menacingly clash Diet Coke cans to put the frighteners on? Sure they did. So did any of us actually end up one millimetre the wiser?

Well, in the end, Mr Lipschitz got out his Bic and sketched a few rough diagrams on the back of a serviette. OK, OK, I know you've paid good money. Here's the low down.

Method

1 Make friends with the vaginal entrance. Get to know its little faults and foibles.
2 Proceed in a womb-wards direction.
3 About a thumb's length up, commence spirited twiddling about.
4 Employ the same motion you'd use to remove clotted Cow & Gate from deep inside a baby's bottle.
5 Persist.
6 Don't give up.
7 Remember Robert the Bruce and the spider.
8 Employ the motion you'd use to open a thermosealed bag of salt 'n' vinegars.
9 Employ the other hand - or you'll end up in casualty with a syndrome known as G-spot finger.
10 Employ a stand-in.

Result

Sod bloody all.

Conclusion

The Lipschitz are liars. No such thing as G-spots.

Proof that G-spots aren't

When I'm not up to my elbows up a chicken's orifice, I present a late night radio programme commonly known as 'The Dirty Weekend Show'. As you might imagine, the prog's scope covers the entire sensual gamut from hot dogs, to doggie-style to letting sleeping dogs lie. So, let me assure you, I haven't shirked G-spots. The problem, of course, is persuading people to expose their G-spotlessness in public. Most of the time, prising a professional sexpert OFF a microphone is no elementary undertaking. They're addicted to proclaiming their status as masterful masturbators, flairful cross-dressers and seasoned chandelier swingers. Mention the G-spot, however, and they plead the Fifth. You can't blame them. Admit they haven't found the damn thing and they stand to forfeit years of hard earned bed cred.

So, I did the sensible thing and threw myself on the mercy of the Gentle Listener. 'Gentle Listener,' quoth I, 'I'm thirty-two and a quarter and still a G-spot virgin. Could anyone out there who's got to grips with their G-spot kindly ring in on 071 224 2000 and share your Genital A–Z with the nation. Did they phone? Let me just say we got more calls when we asked red haired taxidermists from Peckham who'd been abducted by extra-terrestrials to ring in. Is the Gentle Listener normally phone-shy? Well, we had over 300 calls for a competition to win a tea-strainer once used by Barbara Windsor. Does

GOSSIP
GOBBET

Mr. Depp turned out
to have more spots
than me, plus a
hideous Benny from
Crossroads hat and a
foul temper. He was
on an international
tour to publicise his
film *What's Eating
Gilbert Grape?*

Me: 'Are you proud
of the film?'

Mr Depp: 'I don't
know, I haven't seen
it.'

Me: 'If you haven't,
why should we?'

Mr Depp: 'I don't
care if you don't.'

that give you some idea? Once I sprouted a neon zit on my chin the night before I was due to interview 'Hollywood heart-throb Johnny Depp' (Edward Scissorhands to you). I put out an Urgent Acne Advice Radio Alert. By the end of the show 236 pus-squeezers outnumbered 218 leave-well-aloners, but 517 dab-it-with-witch-hazelers carried the vote.

People phone in to discuss the price of condoms, the flavour of condoms, the aroma/size/fashion statement of condoms. They phone to reveal all about premature ejaculation, domination, submission and constipation. They phone to ask me what to wear for their stepmother's parole party. They phone for help with ink spots, grease spots and beauty spots – but they never, ever, not in a year of Sundays, spout a single solitary *bon mot* about G-spots.

Feminist solidarity

Frankly, sisters, it's our bounden duty to find our G-S because boys don't have them. Did you realise that? The G-spot is God's way of making up to us girls for being winkleless. Lord knows, I'm a martyr to penis envy. I've always wanted to put fires out with my pee and dress to the left. Isn't it, therefore, a major swizz that the G-spot, the only women-only erogenous zone – men have sensitive nipples too, silly – is not only in-bloody-visible but im-bloody-possible to put your finger on? (Or anybody else's finger, for that matter.) Just the Almighty having his little joke at our expense again. You'd be forgiven for thinking menstrual cramps, episiotomies and the invention of lycra might have satisfied His celestial need for a good laugh. But you'd be wrong.

What to do if you find your G-spot

Do not, repeat, do not under any circumstances whatsoever write in and tell me all about it. Trumpeting your
erogenous zones all over the show isn't just in poor taste,
it's downright vulgar. G-spots are like Coronation Street,
best partaken of with a quarter of sherbet lemons behind
locked doors. If you are fortunate enough to have a
prominent G-spot for goodness sake, have the grace to
keep it to yourself.

What to do if you can't find your G-spot

Have a helluva fine time looking. Then go down the Job
Centre and find a well hung UB40 with nothing better to
do in the afternoons.

Still searching for his G-spot

Mark Thatcher.

UNLIKELY
PLACES TO
LOCATE
YOUR G-SPOT

• Golders Green
• behind the settee
• church – N.B. Do
  NOT confuse G-spot
  with God-slot.
  Could prove
  embarrassing
• Sainsbury's
• The Jimmy Young
  Show
• Mothercare

☙ 4 ☙

How Many Is Multiple?
2? 12? 32?

Let's hear a big squelching round of sour grapes for multiple orgasms. You've heard all about MOs. They're the sexual carrot the sexperts dangle tantalisingly in front of us gals. Frankly, I'd like to turn it into coleslaw. Multiple orgasms are part of a conspiracy theory specifically evolved to stop women shacking up with poodles, vibrators and chocolate truffle cheesecake and banishing the male organ from our lives.

Here's the theory. Boys scale their sexual peak at eighteen. Five fistfuls before breakfast and they're still rendered Eiffel Tower-like by the suggestive suspension of the 34 bus. It was a case of hard-on, and on, and on and on. Most chaps couldn't walk through the science block without lugging around a pubically placed copy of Gibbon's Decline and Fall. All were fully paid up members of the Masturbating Into Milk Bottles Club – first one to produce a pinta gets the fiver. All were desperate to sperm their way into some female's affections.

Meanwhile, what were we females doing? Waiting. Some of us still are. We of the rarer sex, soothe the sexperts, just have to hang on a little longer. Seventeen sodding years longer to be exact. Seventeen years of peaklessness. Seventeen years of finally plucking up the courage to say: 'Not there; there' seconds before he grunts, leans over for the remote control and deposits us, unclimaxed, in the damp patch. But, hey, say the sexperts, it'll be well worth the wait, ladies, because the very split second we hit our thirties we hurtle crash! bang! wallop! into major league multiple orgasm time. Oh yeah? Well, I'm thirty-two and a quarter and I'm not even guaranteed a flipping single!

What I'd like to know is what exactly qualifies as a multiple orgasm anyway? I mean, how many is multiple? Are we talking more than one a week? More than one a day? More than one at once? If we're talking concurrently running climaxes, the key question is how long is an individual orgasm? Has anyone done the stop watch test? Glenn Close managed two and a half full minutes of gasps, facial contortions and table banging in *Fatal Attraction*. Mine don't last any longer than your average sneeze. Half a second, tops! Most of the time I'm hard pushed not to peg out before the second 'Yes!' of the 'Yes! Yes!' Could it be then, that the world is populated by fraudulent multiple orgasm claimants? Maybe some lucky women, blessed with God-given extra-long Os assume they're achieving multi-plicity when, technically speaking, it's just that their singles last a little longer than average.

Anyway, how do you know when one orgasm becomes many? Do multiples go: 'Explosive earth movement. Stop. Interval. Hiatus. Lull. Pause. Explosive earth movement.' Or do they go: 'Explosive earth movement/explosive earth movement.' In other words, when does one become two? Who is to say when, precisely, one middling to long orgasm vaults the demarcation line and turns into a duo? Have official studies been conducted with white coated stop-watch wielders typing orgasm duration data into their Apple Macs?

A couple of matters have me concerned.

1   How do the seriously serially orgasmic actually tot up how many multiples they're having. Coital calculators? In my case, I have to concentrate so hard on fantasy number 7 (smoked salmon, Denzel Washington and a two-way mirror, since you ask) just to make it to number one, I wouldn't want to risk opening my eyes, let alone keeping a running tally. 'Whoops, there goes number 6. Tense thighs for number 7.'

2   More bewilderingly still, how do their long suffering partners bear UP for the proceedings? Are they:

   a   quite literally bored RIGID

   b   so pissed off with being human orgasmatrons they don't feel like coming

   c   on their fifth anti-ejaculatory recitation of the seven times table?

N.B. There's always the remote possibility that we've been multipling away for years without twigging. How do we find out? We can't. Why? Because no-one exactly knows what constitutes a MO. Why not? Because I don't think anyone exactly has them. So, why doesn't anyone say so? Because we don't dare admit it. Multiple orgasms are the Emperor's New Clothes of sexuality. The most over-hyped non-events of the century. They're a cynical sales gambit, dreamed up by professional sexperts to heighten our feelings of inadequacy and increase dependence on their spurious advice. It's a stratagem that works brilliantly. We've all shelled out for shelves groaning with horny 'How To' books. 'Here a twiddle, there a tickle – hey presto, you're chain-orgasmic.' Give me a break.

They're pedalling pure fantasy. It's lucrative stuff, though. Multiple-Os are such nice little earners any sexpert keen on Kenzo would be a twit not to devote at least one chapter to 'Coaxing the Consecutive Climax'. Think about it. Everyone wants 'em. No-one has the first clue how to achieve 'em. Everyone assumes everyone else is coming/coming/coming right through EastEnders.

And they've got us by the short and curlies. When the MOs don't materialise we should demand a refund. Instead, like the naked Emperor's courtiers, we automatically assume the fault lies with us. Insecurity, thy name is woman. Madonna's 'Erotic' is a grossly inappropriate anthem for female-kind. 'Neurotic' would be just the job. We're so sexually insecure, we won't risk blowing the gaffe on the non-existent MO, just in case the rest of the planet is well stuck into simultaneous climax number 17 and rising.

Multiple orgasms are a pivot of popular mythology. The other night, relecting that the afterglow lasts somewhat longer than the glow itself, I flicked on the TV. Unless you count a prehistoric Cagney and Lacey, there was no alternative to the alternative comedian. He was well into his sex-with-an-older-woman routine. 'You know what they're like, these mature ladies?' Nods, winks, howls of appreciative laughter from audience. 'Darling, I'm coming.' He rolled his eyes and panted. The audience roared ecstatically. 'You tie a knot in your condom, light a cigarette, she's still at it.' He hyperventilated and gasped. The audience wet its collective Wranglers. 'You nip off to make yourself a Caesar salad, a Bloody Mary and some popcorn. Pop your head round the bedroom door and she's still going strong.' He bucked, writhed, wriggled and chucked in a couple of 'Oh My Gods'. The audience guffawed.

I practically threw up. It was sickeningly obvious that the

audience was serially orgasmic to a (wo)man. They had to be, or they wouldn't have got the gag. An auditorium full of non-multiples would have been gawping blankly in mute incomprehension, not chortling their self-satisfied heads off. 'Bugger it and blast it!' thought I. 'Josephine bloody Public is peaking and I'm not.' And then I remembered that if anyone had been watching me, I'd have belly laughed with the best of them. Not because I'm multiply-orgasmic, but because I don't want to look like a sexually retarded nincompoop. I don't believe a soul in that sniggering audience had ever sailed close to the winds of multiple-dom. They chortled from fear not familiarity. It takes courage to stay shtum when all about you are losing theirs.

I'm a lot cosier in the closet, but I'm coming out. I've never had an MO. What's more, no-one in my immediate family has either – there's hard fact for you. Just for the record, I owned up to my orgasmic inadequacies in *SHE* Magazine and a charming reader called Sue Leffley of Leeds sent in the following indispensable advice.

'Speaking as an occasional "multi", I have some advice for Vanessa: get on top, and get in control! All you need is plenty of foreplay, lots of lust and one male flat on his back. Climb aboard and ride. After orgasm number one, take a few deep breaths and keep on – if your man can control himself long enough, you can enjoy several orgasms. Good luck!'

So far, so so, but if Sue Leffley of Leeds can manage it, hope springs maternal. I hope I'm wrong. I desperately want to believe in the tooth fairy, living happily ever after and multiple orgasms. I'm dying for the second coming.

A
Few
Home
Truths

5

If God Had Meant Us To Lick Them, Surely They'd Have Chocolate On The Top

All right, I confess, I can't stomach oral sex. Affectionate though I undoubtedly feel towards the willy that sired my children, I haven't the remotest desire to lick it. Not that I object to giving it a friendly pat once in a while. It's just chomping upon the thing that leaves me deep frozen. The pillock who said: ''Tis better to give than to receive' definitely wasn't of the female persuasion. Receiving is like finding a forgotten packet of Maltesers in your pocket – quite extraordinarily delightful. What's more, most men can't talk with their mouths full so, for once, our fantasies soar heavenward in gruntless instruction-free silence. Tongues, it must also be said, are so much more subtle than winkles. As far as I'm concerned, any woman lucky enough to lock labia with a happy lapper has her own personal passport to paradise.

Frankly I'd rather give blood than give head – at least you get a plate of custard creams and a nice cup of tea afterwards. I'm convinced if God had meant us to lick them, he'd have put a blob of Galaxy on the top. Let me just burst right out of the closet and say it: 'Willies don't taste particularly cordon bleu.' Let's face it, a penis is not a spring roll. There are a multitude of things you might want to do with a penis, but sinking your teeth into it is not one. You don't glimpse the helmet protruding pinkly from a paisley boxer short and think 'Yum!' Even the freshest possible, straight from the shower, strictly smegma-free penis, permeated from stem to stern with the clean, tangy fragrance of Imperial Leather still falls chronically short of a gastronomic banquet. By the same token, musty, fusty members that have spent the last eight hours chafing sweatily against the inside fly of a Levi's 501 are hardly likely to set your salivary glands a-gush.

In short, you can feel remarkably drawn towards a particular penis without ever once experiencing the slightest urge to join it at the lip. Just as you might spend decades cherishing a Spode cow creamer lovingly bequeathed by a maiden aunt, without once inclining towards trying it for taste. I've only met one woman who claimed to enjoy oral sex and she was a protein-deficient vegan. Bar those first incandescent moments when you're so consumed with lust – you'd use your tongue to excavate his nostrils if he so much as hinted at it – there's no denying the fact that women perform oral sex strictly for charitable reasons. There's absolutely nothing in it for us – except, of course, the obvious, see next Chapter. We don't have sexually responsive nerve endings in our teeth. There's no direct line of sensory stimulation linking our gums to our genitals. So, when you dish up spotted dick, for heaven's sake don't kid yourselves you're doing us any favours. Remember. You owe us one. Plus interest.

Note to suckees

We are not, do not, and never have enjoyed mouth to dick resuscitation. Linda Lovelace was an actress. *Deep Throat* was almost as authentic as *E.T.* Women who moan: 'Let me get my tongue round your ice-cream cone, Big Boy!' usually have heroin habits/expensive pimps to support. I admit that once, ten years ago on a snowy Edgware eve, when my parents were out, I told an ex I couldn't wait to put tongue to tip. I didn't mean it, OK? I also said I worshipped Manchester United, bungee jumping, and all his friends. I didn't mean that either. I also said his Mother was 'an interesting and formidable lady'. I knew she was an ugly old bitch first time I laid eyes on the clapped-out sow.

You know we said we liked it, we were lying

So please spare us all that garbage about: 'I can't understand why you don't want to, Petal. You used to enjoy it so much.' Actually we were concentrating on not gagging all over the Wilton but:

a   everyone else was getting married, our mothers were itching to book the hall and we couldn't wait to start picking out a matching dinner service
b   we'd read *Cosmo* so we thought every other female on the planet preferred a mouthful of penis to pralines'n' cream Baskin Robbins.

N.B. When it comes to faking it, women don't stop at mere orgasms.

Note to suckers

Performing oral sex is at best chokingly tedious, at worst jaw achingly retch-worthy. Either the penis sticks there – a stagnant banana – forcing you to bob up and down like a nodding mandarin, or it thrusts in and out, at perilous risk to your crown and bridge work. In both cases, it's a definite example of biting off more than you can chew. Ladies' mouths weren't designed to accommodate erections. I personally have terrible trouble fitting in a Cadbury's Creme Egg. No woman would never attempt to devour a whole salami. She'd sensibly reach for the cleaver and cut it into wafer thin slices. Unfortunately, circumcision aside, willies are unsliceable. Vaginas are elastic. Mouths are not. It'll never be a comfortable fit. Practising with gob-stoppers to train up your over-bite doesn't work. Nor does signing up with a dentist who keeps yelling 'Open wide!' What to do? Refuse through gritted teeth.

The hidden weapon

Men are terrified of teeth. They catch your Colegate ring of confidence glinting in the recessed lighting and their testicles shrivel. It takes balls to place your balls at the mercy of some woman's incisor. So fellatio is always tinged with terror. Half the charm of chancing their yard-arm is that, at any moment, you just might bite. You've heard of running scared. Welcome to coming scared. Of course, this is great news for reluctant suckers. If he's blocking up your airways, asphyxia's imminent and you'd rather be descaling the kettle anyway, simply bring your molars into play. Commence with a few playful nips. Then follow through with the sort of force you'd use to break into a shiny new Granny Smith. He'll yank away that organ so fast it whistles.

You suck mine and I'll . . .

Oral sex is only worth bothering with on a quid pro quo basis. 'Relationships', say the pundits, 'are all about give and take.' Absolutely – giving and taking head. This is the point where committed Anglo-Saxons who've never been more Mediterranean than Bournemouth suddenly come over desperately Français. For some reason *soixante-neuf* isn't nearly as rude as 69. I can't pretend to understand it. You don't catch couples in East Finchley asking '*Un* egg, or *deux*, darling?' or address mail (except, possibly, French letters) to *vingt et un*, Cherry Tree Lane. Tis only au sujet de blow jobs and surrounding districts that lifelong Franco-phobes lapse into strangulated frog. Anyway, the great secret of successful *soixante-neuf* is not to be much shorter/taller than your partner. Roughly equi-distant genitals avoid cricks in the neck, hunched shoulders and all manner of unsightly contortions.

Note to female novices

1 Yes, it is called a blow job but don't.

Note to male novices

1 Applying a clothes peg to the nose is not appropriate, unless you have a letter from your GP.
2 Part the ways first with a forefinger. Pubes between the teeth are a devil to shift and running off mid-lick to dig out the dental floss could be a slight mood dampener.

Recipe for a palatable penis

Mask that yesterday's Y-front taste by dipping afore-mentioned member in:

SWEET
a Häagen Dazs (Belgian Chocolate infinitely superior): might wilt a fraction with first chill-factor shock, vigorous suction should revive.

b Fortnum & Mason pipless raspberry jam. Do not economise and spoon on a spot of Hartleys. If you do, you cheapskate, the pips will pop up in all kinds of uncomfortable places.

c Whipped Cream – I always hand whip, but plebian practitioners favour those unpleasant aerosol cans of UHT and E Numbers.

d Golden Syrup – death to duvet covers, old towels a necessity.

e Tiramisu – what's a culinary cliché between chums.

SAVOURY

Too disgusting to contemplate, although I have a chum who swears by Dolmio with garlic and basil.

Ladies, what if you get really good and the inevitable happens?

Turn to the next page and find out.

❧ 6 ❧

The Great Swallowing Debate
(Or, Make Mine A Diet Coke,
Hold The Penis Colada!)

The problem with giving too many blow jobs is that you might just get good at it. Perfect your suction technique and the inevitable happens. Asti Spermanti. Yeeuch! Remember Biology O level? Giant electric blue ovaries, fearsome Fallopian tubes and dollops of sperm under a microscope? Even Walt Disney couldn't prettify semen. Mickey Mouse, Donald Duck and Sammy Sperm? No way. Even if you give it long eyelashes, twinkly green eyes and a tulip behind the ear, semen's still horrible yoghurty stuff swarming with billions of squiggly tadpoles, rather like a stagnant puddle bustling with blowfly larvae. Hardly puts you in the mood to stick a couple of parasols and half a pineapple in it and call it Penis Colada, does it? Given the choice between swigging squirtings of fresh spermatozoa or knocking back a few gallons of Shell Unleaded Premium, most women would opt for the one that comes with tokens towards a nice pyrex pie dish.

Let's talk acceptable beverages here. British tap water is everyone else's urine sprayed with chemicals, irradiated and recycled. Endlessly. Ultimately we're all incestuously sipping stuff that's already been peed out six or seven times by our own grandparents, for God's sake. Diet sodas are a noxious mixture of carcinogenic waste and industrial effluent. Milk is full of sinister hormones pumped in to quell any cow-like instincts in Daisy and the herd. Apple juice transforms innocent children into special effects from *Terminator 2*. So, measured against the contents of your average family fridge, is a few heaped tablespoons of semen really worth making much fuss over? Should we just keep a curved upper lip and take the medicine?

If we could slip in a heaped tablespoonful of sugar to help it go down, maybe there'd be room for negotiation. If not, forget it. Let's be brutally honest. Semen is not Seven Up. Men don't come in five fruit flavours. Even with a heavy cold, it's impossible to convince yourself that male ejaculate is bursting with tangy flavoursome zest. I've been thirty-two and a quarter years in the closet, but the time has arrived to come out and say it: SEMEN TASTES DISGUSTING. I'm talking worse than school dinners. Worse than NHS gynaecology ward spam fritters. Worse than any nutritional torture maliciously devised by British Rail. Sometimes reminiscent of salted glue – don't ask how I know – sometimes runny and revoltingly viscous; sperm is nausea and it happens in disconcertingly unpredictable spurts.

Oral sex and the Jewish question

Actually, I was once asked by the BBC to take part in a programme entitled: Oral Sex – The Last Taboo. My husband couldn't resist a swingeing: 'How the hell would you know?' Bless him! Anyway, it seemed I'd been selected to play my traditional role as Jewish sexpert on hereditary hotline from Freud because the first question they asked was: 'Do Jewish men perform cunnilingus?' No, it's not an Irish airline. So I had to tell the truth. Jewish men do not, will not and never have performed cunnilingus. Why? Because their mothers have told them never to eat anything foreign unless it's been boiled first to get rid of germs.

The second question was direct and to the point: 'Do Jewish women swallow?' And I was happy to enlighten them here, because, after all, this question highlights one of the foremost dilemmas of our era. We don't, because we haven't had the answer to this major theological conundrum: IS SPERM KOSHER? Wriggly little tadpole-type things? I wouldn't be too sure. Until a team of rabbis comes up with the definitive pronouncement, I think we should just play safe and stick to gefilte fish balls (best part of the fish).

Oral sex as part of a slimming diet

Of course, there's many a slip twixt mouth and tip, and it's vital to confront the salient issues. There's more than just instant gratification at steak, sorry stake, here. Call me food fixated, but I've always wanted to know, and I'm sure I speak for generations of women when I demand an answer. IS SPERM FATTENING? How many carbohydrates in a typical ejaculation? Believe me, I've scoured dozens of diet books, but I've never seen the number of calories per emission listed. Seriously, semen may be major league fat food. A second on the lips, a lifetime on the hips. For *crème brûlée*, I'd risk it. But for that porridgey puree? Dream on.

Oral sex and the high protein diet

Sperm may be yukky – 'Ugh!', 'Eeeurch!', 'Aargh' and 'Phthphth!' are a random sample of reactions to my random survey in which I asked a random selection of women who happened to be queueing to use our neighbourhood Barclay's Bank cashpoint how they felt about the taste – but, have you ever considered that it might be good for you? Stands to reason, if medicine isn't absolutely revolting it definitely isn't doing you any good; likewise semen. Talk about Sperm U Like. Next time you think about swabbing it off with a Kleenex, pause and reflect. Jism is a perfect balance of protein, amino acids (whatever they may be) and all the esoteric, hard-to-come-by vitamins you can usually only get in Jerusalem artichoke peelings. Try taking a deep breath and swallowing for England. You'll be amazed at the strengthening effect on your cuticles.

What's the alternative?

One swallow may very well not make a summer, but not swallowing poses appalling problems of bedroom etiquette. I mean, if you don't just drink the stuff down, what the heck do you do with it? The options are few and gruesome.

1   Spit it out. But where? Spitting into a handy receptacle isn't the world's most erotic tableau. And there's always the danger that the kids/dog/au pair'll mistake it for Evian in the morning! Anyway, the night/day (I don't know how debauched you are) will inevitably arrive

when the handy receptacle isn't handy. Do you then:

a   Spit straight on to the bedside table. It was only from John Lewis, and anyway the insurance should cover it.

b   Spit straight on to the carpet. The children have done worse. And if they haven't, the dog has.

c   Grit your teeth and belt at full tilt towards the bathroom, then give vent in the sink.

N.B. One of my best friends who shall be nameless (Lydia), insisted on having an *en suite* installed to cut down total running/spitting time.

2   Pass the aforementioned semen into your lover's own mouth via a kiss, Swedish style. In my limited experience this is likely to result in a fit of furious coughing, gagging and spluttering on his part, guaranteed to shatter that pre-coital glow.

3   Whip your head away and take the blast full in the cheek. My sources tell me sperm makes a formidable facepack. Allow to harden and leave on for fifteen minutes for emphatically tightened pores. Be sure, however, to credit Estée Lauder, if anyone asks.

4   Allow it to dribble down your chin and on to your breasts and encourage your partner to massage said liquid into your breasts. (You can tell I've been alone and frustrated in too many characterless hotel rooms watching Red Hot Dutch. But, what the heck?)

❦ **7** ❦

My Mish Posish Wish
(Or, Lads On Top, What A Flop!)

You know the missionary who invented the missionary position? Well, I hope a bunch of voracious cannibals stuffed a sizeable wodge of sage and onion up his proverbials and spit-roasted him very slowly over a low light. Or alternatively chopped him up with a handful of oregano and turned him into T.S. Eliot's recipe: 'a nice little, white little missionary stew'. How do I know he was a he? Because female anatomy and the mish posish don't mesh, that's how. Mrs Missionary was probably too knackered reclaiming native souls from purgatory to say so, but her husband should have stuck to Holy Communion.

The mish posish, frequently referred to as 'the rabbinical position' in my neck of the suburbs, should be known as The Curse of Coitus. We're bombarded, not to mention bamboozled, by statistics telling us what we know all too miserably well already. Penetrative sex leaves most women auditioning for Findus. Why? Because we're pinioned to the double posture springing by a fourteen stone weakling and *Last Tango In Paris* it bloody isn't. Eight out of ten women never climax AT ALL during intercourse. Eight out of ten women are only keeping awake by doing a mental sprint through the lyrics of 'American Pie' during intercourse. Eight out of ten women can achieve all on their own with a hairbrush handle what their men can't manage in a month of Friday nights during intercourse. And the other two women are liars!

From the female perspective – usually underneath – sexual intercourse is a damp squib. He can huff and he can puff, but he'll never actually locate your house, let alone blow the damn thing down. The clitoris is God's second little joke against womankind. (See G-spots, Chapter 3, for the first.) Let the Germaines, Camilles and Naomi Wolves strut their sisterhood supremacy stuff. The Almighty is sniggering into a handy cloud. Even before Eve nibbled at that Orange Pippin, He'd made extra double certain sure she was already being punished.

Sexperts are forever making clitoral/penile comparisons. The clitoris, they tell us is actually a penis in miniature – a fabulous tiny tool, literally fizzing with erectile tissue. Hard ons? We got 'em. Sensitive tip? We got it. Ejaculatory mechanism? We got that too. There's just one itsy bitsy teeny weeny problem. WE CAN'T FIND IT.

The whole point about penises is that they aren't miniature. And if they are their owners have the good grace to keep them hidden in their M & S Y-fronts. Infant males start masturbating before they've even been, as Miriam Stoppard would say, 'introduced to solids'. 'Baby, meet pureed carrot.' 'Pureed carrot, may I present Baby?' It doesn't take brains, tenacity, a compass, a torch or a demon sex-drive to find a penis. Men of all ages testify to the fact that the penile shaft is the hand's natural resting place. Why do you think most males take so naturally to driving a stick shift? They've been perfecting the necessary hand gestures all their lives.

There's nothing on earth more attention seeking than a

HELLO
DOWN THERE!

A GUIDE

penis. They dangle, wobble, bob up and down at inopportune moments, leak, ooze – everything but glow green in the dark. The clitoris, on the other hand – don't let me mislead you, it isn't actually ON the other hand – is a self-effacing, introspective, socially inept little organ. Publicity shy? Are you kidding? The clitoris is a genital Garbo. Repeat after me: 'The question before us is where's my clitoris.' Say it fast and it rhymes, but that's no consolation. At this very moment, there are grown women all over the Home Counties who can whip up a convincing salmon en croûte, rag-roll an eighteenth-century butter-churn and turn table napkins into waterlilies, who still haven't established even a passing acquaintance with their fun buttons. After all, the clitoris is somewhere 'down there', and 'down there' isn't an area one feels quite comfortable delving about in.

While it's undeniably true that certain feminist awareness groups spend entire evenings communing with their own vaginas by means of intelligently positioned mirrors – Every Monday, 6 p.m.: LEARN TO LOVE YOUR LABIA EVENING – most of us are on no more than brisk daily soaping terms with our front bottoms. Our inter-vaginal relationship is strictly formal, a quick wash and brush up, a tampon or two. In short, if you showed a woman 5000 pictures of isolated eyebrows she'd have no hesitation homing in on her own. Slap down 5000 polaroids of assorted isolated clits, and she'd have trouble sorting hers out from from Edwina Currie's.

So, we're agreed, you don't just happen upon a clitoris. It's not like bumping into your old science teacher in Budgens. Clitoral contact can never be accidental because, even in broad daylight, using a fluorescent Bic and teams of trained sniffer dogs, the clitoris is an absolute bastard to find. Once unearthed, a clit needs wooing. You can't simply jab a stubby forefinger into it and expect Perry Como to erupt into Magic Moments. A clitoris must be coerced, nay cajoled into participation. We're talking direct pressure in the most indirect way. Think fluttering feathers. Think tickling tassels. Think anything alliterative you have the energy for. The trick is gentle consistency and consistent gentleness. Thrust at a clit and it jellifies and goes into retirement.

The mish posish unveiled

What do women want from intercourse? Altogether now: 'Gentle, but consistent pressure on the clitoris.' What do women get from the mish posish?

1 The full weight of your partner's paunch.
2 Hot.
3 Pins and needles.
4 Dissatisfied with the ceiling paintwork.
5 Very little else.

Why? Because:

1 It rubs against the wrong bit.
2 Even if you stick a pillow under your bum and squeeze your thighs together it still rubs against the wrong bit.
3 We've all read the articles that say 'indirect pressure from below should do the trick' but they're nothing but fanciful bollocks.
4 Even if you were an anatomical marvel and it DID happen to rub against the RIGHT bit, it would rub:
   a too hard
   b too short

CLITORAL CLUES

1 If it's hairy it isn't a clitoris.
2 If it's one of a matching pair it isn't a clitoris.
3 If it's covered with an 'I Love Mum' tattoo, it probably isn't a clitoris.
4 If it bites the hand that feeds it, it isn't a clitoris.
5 If it's cold and wet, it might well be the dog's nose, but it definitely isn't a clitoris.
6 If it comes free with a packet of Frosties it's quite unlikely to be a clitoris.
7 If it comes with pine effect brackets from B & Q it could be a clitoris, but, trust me, you don't want it.

41

So here's what I wish for the mish posish, capisce?

1   It should be declared illegal between consenting adults (except on Saturday nights when you're so knackered you, to be perfectly frank, can't be fagged with the finer points).

2   Indulging in the mish posish should be a fineable offence. All fines to be paid in cash to the reluctant mish positionee.

3   All overhead mirrors should be removed prior to commencing the mish posish. An aerial view of jiggling buttocks is only a marginal improvement on Emmerdale Farm.

4   Full Valet Service, to include finger/tongue/toe variations to be available post afterglow. Pretending to be asleep prohibited.

8

Taking Oneself In Hand

Brits have a habit of hurling insults which ought to be terms of endearment. Take 'Wanker!' for example. I should jolly well hope so too. Good Lord! What's a spilled seed between friends? Let's face it, we're ALL wankers. And, yes, allowing the showerhead/rubber duck/shampoo bottle to become accidentally shipwrecked between your thighs when you're officially rinsing out the Head'n'Shoulders DOES count. So does wearing size 8 Levis while pedalling on an exercise bike. And as for leaning up against the washer/dryer while it's on SPIN? I don't care if you ARE clutching a J-cloth while pretending to squirt the worksurfaces with Vim. It's masturbation delegation, pure and simple. So occasionally your left hand knows perfectly well what your right hand's doing? More power to your digits. You won't get any raps on the knuckles in this book. Strictly *entre nous*, I'm a DIY fan. As I'm sure my Great-Grandfather Feltz, had he spoken English, would have said: 'Taboo? Schmaboo! If it doesn't cost money, doesn't play havoc with your French manicure, and isn't fattening, enjoy!'

The prob here is that masturbation after marriage – look, cohabitors, I couldn't care less; if you're not, you're not – isn't, it seems, an acceptable pastime. It may be top of the conversational pops for third formers at every boys' prep school in the nation. It's a great British tradition that Inter-House Wanking Tournaments appear on every Fixtures List.

'Behind the cricket pavilion, 2 p.m. Drake v Raleigh. First to fill up the milk bottle wins a Curly-Wurly. Pull together for the honour of St Saviours!'

It seems, though, that grown-ups in regular relationships are meant to have something a bit more mutual to occupy them. You try flinging in a nonchalant reference to cross-dressing over the carrot and coriander. I guarantee 75 per cent of the MPs present will ask to borrow your Gossard Ultrabra and the rest of the assembly won't so much as choke on their ciabatta. Dare, however, to toss in (metaphorically speaking) a casual allusion to the M word, and you'll suddenly find yourself quite excruciatingly beyond the pale.

We've come a long way baby. We know having a Barclays (work it out) doesn't make you foam at the mouth in embarrassing locations, put you on the waiting list for a guide dog, or cause huge hairy warts to errupt volcanically on your extremities. (At least we hope not.) No-one in the compassionate 90s would grudge a friend in need a quick, private twiddle of his/her own knobs – provided there wasn't a partner just starboard of the duvet happy to do the twiddling for them. Masturbation, croon the sexperts, is perfectly acceptable as second best. We're quite OK about a spot of self-love (or self-abuse, depending on your dictionary) in the absence of the Real McCoy. It's when the Real McCoy's ready, able and willing with eau de toilette dabbed in all the appropriate places and we still opt to fly solo that the Sexually Correct Lobby flips on to red alert.

When you mention wanking, long-monogs don't swap smouldering glances and dirty giggles. They look startled, then guilty, then faintly pissed off, and then become utterly immersed in a passionate debate about global warming. Why? Because you're not SUPPOSED to want to. Jerking your gherkin is considered a sign of immaturity. Fine. Let me give you a few reliable signs of maturity – hormone replacement therapy, incontinence pads and matching his'n'hers tombstones. Which would you rather be?

Here are the results of the most recent relevant survey, 'Sexual Behaviour in the 1970s'. This (surprise, surprise) American study was based on questionnaires completed by 2,026 people in 24 cities (71 per cent of whom were married). Apparently 72 per cent of husbands masturbate. So do 68 per cent of wives. If you want to know how often, husbands averaged twenty-four times a year, wives only ten. And that was before the recession, when people could still afford to go out for a pizza instead. Proof conclusive that couples who could be swinging companionably from the Habitat paper globe are wanking instead.

Should we be ashamed of ourselves? Should we lament the fact that we're indulging in nasty, covert dabblings behind locked bathroom doors? Should we give it up for Lent? Vow never again to meddle with our fiddly bits without audience participation? Schlep in our husbands and wives every time we get the urge and make the whole thing conjugal? Give me a break! Masturbation may not show much team spirit, but it's vital. I'm talking essential, imperative, absolutely necessary. Wanking isn't what you do INSTEAD of sex with a partner, it's what you do AS WELL. Barring colourful local perversions, there are two distinct kinds of sex operating within marriage. The first is the five star sensual smorgasbord which involves time, emotion and

MASTURBATION:
THE CONS

1 leads to the
unpleasant
arthritic condition
known as
Wanker's Wrist
2 wastes valuable
time and you still
haven't read that
incredibly boring
Stephen Hawking
book you said you
wanted for Xmas
3 wife/husband
might burst
in/wake up in the
middle and catch
you at it
4 storage space
problem: where to
stow collection of
Shaven Ravers so
the hired help
doesn't end up
dusting it?
5 too hands-on

a massive expenditure of energy biting each other's elbows and langorously caressing each toe-nail. The second is quick relief sex. Tube emptying time. You know what I'm talking about. The forty second clit attack that works so much better than a Mogadon. Long-monogs need both. Multiple mutual orgasm – assuming such a phenomenon exists – isn't always the bee's bollocks. Sometimes the whole concept is just too shatteringly knackering.

Full scale sex is like three courses at a Berni Inn. You don't fancy it every night. Occasionally, you yearn for the sexual equivalent of a boil in the bag cod and peas for one. Something, speedy, easy and entirely selfish. Cue masturbation. I know a chap who insists that 'a willie in the hand is worth two in the bush'. 'Any particular bush?' I asked. 'I'm not in the least particular,' he replied. 'You mean you actually prefer it?' I asked, incredulously. 'No contest,' said he. 'Even with your Brenda (who shall be anonymous) all open thighs and heaving 38DDs, aching to subsume your throbbing etcetera?' 'Yep.' 'Why?' 'Because I know what I like.' Granted, he sounds like someone who buys his fine art at Woolworths, but you have to admit, the guy has a point.

Despite all the putrid garbage vomited up by simpering airport novelists, great sex is never instinctive. One man's erogenous zone is another man's no-no. If a tall, dark, rugged aristocrat/stunt-man named Hugo/Brick swept you off on his stallion/Harley Davidson and rogered the living daylights out of you, chances are you'd have to ask him for a hand-job afterwards. Why? Because he wouldn't have the foggiest notion that:

a you can't stand your breasts being tickled
b you can only come if someone's whistling the Marseillaise

Sex is an acquired skill, masturbation, on the other hand, comes naturally. You'd never spend twenty fruitless minutes twirling away at your own earlobe, now would you? You'd bypass non-starters like labia (maj and min) and go straight for the clitty-gritty. Mid-masturbate, you don't find yourself slapping yourself on the wrist and saying 'Take it easy!' do you? You know if you're thirsty. You know if you should have put on a thermal vest. And, you're the only person on earth who really knows how you like to be made love to.

Anyway, is it really fair to foist the entire burden of your genital satiation on your other half? Isn't it a little demanding to insist your partner be responsible for every single one of your orgasms from here to eternity, and re-grout the bathroom tiles as well? Don't shirk your share of the workload. If he's got a board meeting/hernia/hangover, bung him a couple of Panadol and go it alone.

MASTURBATION:
THE PROS

1 if you change hands it feels like sex with a stranger
2 saves valuable time, and you might get round to that fascinating Stephen Hawking book
3 wife/husband might burst in/wake up in the middle, catch you at it, get mightily turned on and do the same
4 you might get lucky and collide with your G-spot
5 only yourself to worry about

9

Sexual Adventure
(Or, How Do You Get
Taramasalata Stains Off The
Laura Ashley)

If you want to flog billions of books, two words will guarantee you at least a week's lucrative sojourn on *The Sunday Times* top ten sellers list. The first is DIET. 'The Princess Di Chuck It Up Diet', 'The Eggplant and Enema Diet', 'The Angus Deayton Designer Suit Satire Diet', Margaret Thatcher's 'Downing Street: The Fat Free Years'. Publishing cynics shamelessly exploit our cellulite phobia. With Kate and her Mossketeers strutting their skeletons on the world's catwalks, even emaciated crispbread nibblers are convinced they're obscenely obese. Flesh is the nation's favourite foe. We all know the truth. Dieting makes you fat. Fat is a feminist issue. But we don't care. We want IN. IN is THIN. So we need to believe that size 10 Calvin Klein's are only a few pages away. Diet books are hope made concrete. We see. We buy. We lose five pounds. We gain seven. We blame Diet Book A, and plonk down the cash for Diet Book B. We're investing in a dream. And if it stuffs the naturally skinny author's lycra work-out gear with fat wads of our cash, we don't begrudge it – much!

I don't need to tell you the second word that shifts books. It also shifts cars, chocolate, double frigging glazing, kitchen sodding units, in-bloody-surance, and every single consumable from patio furniture to coffins. Vegetarian hamburgers? Bung in a walnut, celery stick, bit of boob, a hint of nips and a couple of buttocks. Goldfish bowls? Have them borne aloft by a bevy of topless mermaids with squiggles of plastic seaweed at cleavage level. Tampax? Home in on bouncing bottoms in unbloodied leotards. Lavatory cleaner? Make sure Mrs Average Housewife tackles that turd stained bowl with her above average Bristols straining at the seams of her Woman At C & A T-shirt.

Sex sells, but not quite as well as sex + insecurity. Bugger the ozone layer. When we're not fretting about blanc-mange thighs and marshmallow bums, we're torturing ourselves mercilessly about The Other. Heavens, we've watched the Gold Blend ad. We're absolutely sure we should be simmering with barely controllable lust at all points of the twenty-four hour clock. Even Granada's Mr Boring, Ken 'Make mine polyester' Barlow regularly gets his end away with floozies who're no better than they should be. Meanwhile, not only are we not having much sex (bar Friday nights and public holidays), we're not really missing it. Given the option we'd far rather colour co-ordinate our partner's socks, brew up vats of bol. for the freezer, or make some headway with the Antirrhinums.

We've been weaned on *Cosmopolitan* founder Helen Gurley Brown's *Having It All* philosophy. We may be quite happy not having it very much, but happiness isn't the point. If cataclysmic climaxes, expense account careers, characterful table-centres and bathrooms with that quirky 'zing' are ours for the taking, we've only ourselves to blame if we don't reach out and grab 'em. So we're suckers for books that tell us how to be better suckers. We know we've only our rotten, flabby, slothful selves to blame if we don't have great sex three times before our 6 a.m. grapple with the rowing machine.

The books that sell up the most turbulent storm belong to the 'How To Spice Up Your Love Life' genre. The implication is simple. 'You've been doing it wrong. You're lousy in bed and it's your own stupid fault. Do as I say and you'll turn into an insatiable sex machine.' Do they work? Very nicely thank you for the sexperts who wrote them. Do they actually put lead in your HB? Give over! Let's be blunt. You've been together so long, there are cave paintings of your first date. The poor chap's seen you through two labours, chicken pox, slippery Dutch caps, and bad hair days. As far as he's concerned, the only bits of your anatomy with any modicum of mystique still attached are the liver and lungs. No book, even if it did set him back £16.99 in hardback, is going to whip him into a state of frenzy at the sight of your tired and emotional bosoms. No book, even if it does have full colour illustrations of athletic couples shagging the shoulder pads off one another in the horse and cart position, is going to incite you to attempt such tomfoolery. And no book, even with a foreword by Paula Yates, is going to induce you to ring him at work and growl: 'Hurry home, Hunky, and sniff my knickers.'

The trouble with sexperts is that they're desperately limited. Think about it. There are only a finite number of orifices, and most of those are no earthly use. You won't get much joy sticking a penis down your earhole or even up your nose (not to mention your navel) so it pretty much boils down to mouths and front/back bottoms. Given the fact that we're also somewhat fettered on the fidelity front

– importing double jointed twins and a fire-eater might do wonders for our sex-lives, but it's hardly back to basics – they're well and truly up against it. Picture the scene. You're a sexpert and you've just banked a sizeable advance which has paid off the mortgage on your little bolt-hole in Britanny. Now you're stuck in front of the infernal word processor trying to think up *205 Ways To Make Every Night Honeymoon Night*. What do you do? If you've any sense, you find a starving English Literature undergraduate and slip him twenty-five quid a week in cash to ghost write the damn thing. Failing that, you fall back on the sexpert's staples.

Staple 1:
position is all

Sexperts are just like estate agents. Both species pretend to be convinced that position is everything. Sexperts insist that if copulation between the covers doesn't grab you, slinging one leg in the fridge and the other in the biscuit tin definitely will. Why on earth they think the body that fails to inflame your vitals lying bottie down, will suddenly send you wild with desire lying bottie up, is beyond me? Maybe they figure you'll be so busy trying to make genital contact without falling downstairs and frightening the goldfish, you won't have a chance to realise you're not demented with ecstasy? When other people are hungover, they have the sense to belch at the television while telling their AlkaSeltzer to 'Quiet down, you bastard!' When sexperts are hungover, they devise insanely bizarre sexual positions and foist them on to us.

There's no end to the hallucinogenic physical jerks these professional mythmakers dredge up to torment us.

EXAMPLES OF
BIZARRE SEXUAL
POSITIONS

- The spoons (also known as the cutlery position).
- The mortar and pestle.
- The wheelbarrow.
- The yoghurt pot.
- Doggie style.
- Froggy style.
- Gerbil style.
- The Hurricane Higgins.
- The Big Mac.
- The Lord Lucan.

RESULT?

Fractured limbs. Fractured furniture. Slipped discs. Ripped slips. Groin strain. Brain strain.

NET EFFECT?

Off sex for lengthy restorative convalescence.

Staple 2:
location, location, location

When sexperts run out of positions, they fixate on locations. They'd have us fornicating alfresco, in leaf-dappled sylvan settings and under dripping urban spiggots. They'd like us atop the kitchen table, astride the privet, in the coat cupboard and in boxes at the Albert Hall. They recommend other people's apple orchards, the backs of taxis; lifts, mid-floor, with your bottom pushed up against the 'Door Closed' sign; cemeteries; cinemas, and any kind of loo. I don't know why, but sexperts are passionately devoted to the idea of sex in toilets. After all, they invented the Mile High Club, members of which have embedded members in aeroplane khazis. Call me old-fashioned, but urine soaked floors, excremental odours and crumpled tissues do less than Terry Wogan for my libido.

Their premise is that escaping the bedroom will unleash your adolescent ardour. Exchanging your cosy sheets for a cow-patted crevasse will send the blood gurling to your vitals. I say: 'If he can get it at home anyway, what the hell's the point of risking splinters in his testicles?'

RESULT?

Halfway through pastoral frolic sprayed with pesticide by

vocal local yokel. Coital photograph appears in local press. Lose job/pension/sense of humour.

NET EFFECT?

Off sex for foreseeable future.

I decided to try this 'Spice Up Your Sex-Life' malarky last Monday. I had every intention of bursting forth upon an unspecting spouse, dragging him into the airing cupboard and smearing sandwich spread all over his unmentionables. But Daughter 1 had a temperature and Daughter 2 had a spelling test. By the time I'd Calpoled, and 'i' before 'e' except after 'c'd, aforementioned spouse was snoring with the remote control on his chest and the au pair had polished off the sandwich spread.

So much for sexual adventure.

❧ 10 ❧

Keeping Your Mind On The Job (Or, When You've Finished, The Ceiling Could Do With A Nice Coat of Magnolia)

You recognise the moment. The Big O's hovering promisingly just around the corner. The rhythm's an intoxicating combo of foxtrot and reggae with spontaneous outbreaks of Highland fling. The pressure on your most sensitive pinnacle's practically perfect. When suddenly, a lurid vision of tomorrow night's turkey, still sitting pretty in the freezer, deep frozen to its very giblets, pops, unbidden into your brain. Instantly, your nipples deflate. Determined not to kiss that climax goodbye without a fight, you attempt to redirect your grey matter with a couple of swift commands. 'Think Richard Gere's rear!' 'Think Bill Clinton in the buff!' Unfortunately, it's not that simple. Your partner's still thrusting his socks off, but the Big O's disappearing over the horizon. 'Half defrosted bird = eight nearest and dearest with salmonella,' you ponder as your clitoris turns to jelly. 'Do I risk microwaving it? Or play safe with M & S chicken kiev?' Judging by the grunts, Hubbie's grinding up to fifth gear. Just then, surprise, surprise, he subsides into substandard snorts, rolls over, stuffs what looks like a pale pink cotton wool ball into his pyjamas and splutters something apologetic about being 'OK until I remembered Tuesday's presentation to that Danish company in front of Old Simpson'.

Sex is like classical music: death to civilised conversation, impossible to hum along with and you never know what you're supposed to be thinking about while it's going on. Occasionally, lovemaking transports us to a cerebral stratosphere as we coast towards ecstasy in harmony with the gentle thud of clashing pubic bones. Most of the time, though, it's one of life's toughest challenges just keeping our minds on the job. Let's face it, for a working woman, sex represents the closest she's come all day to five (OK three and a half) minutes' peace, with her feet up. Naturally, she uses that tranquil interlude in life's manic agenda to collect her thoughts. And what an eclectic collection! They're Virginia Woolfian stream of consciousness with bits of electric blue. Here's a recent example: 'Oooh, that feels fab. Aaah, I love a long wet tongue in my ear. And those new earrings I picked up at Fenwicks go brilliantly with my navy jacket. Or are they too tarty? Or aren't they tarty enough? Cunnilingus? Must be a late birthday present. Slurp. Slurp. God, he sounds hungry. Which reminds me I'd better make a tart for Saturday's supper. Will I fondle his balls? he asks. Are plums in season? What? Finished already?' My best friend, who'll murder me if I tell you her name (Deborah), claims to have devised the entire living room colour scheme while in the missionary position. I can trump that without even trying. Last week, my husband hit the jackpot and I screamed 'Verruca!' No, it isn't the Yiddish pronunciation of 'Eureka!' I'd just realised that the tenacious lump on my four-year-old's foot wasn't a gob of last week's chewing gum.

Thinking of England

This has a warm, nostalgic ring, rather like biting into a slice of hot buttered Hovis. What's more, it isn't as asexual as you might assume. Patriotism can be aphrodisiac. This sceptred isle isn't all High Barnet and Eastbourne, you know. There's always steamy Soho, sordid Bloomsbury and Gucci-trodden Knightsbridge to generate your juices. Some women of my acquaintance are still eminently susceptible to all points phallic. Just imagine mounting Centre Point, Scafell Pyke, Ely Cathedral or Jodrell Bank and you'll find the result eminently gratifying.

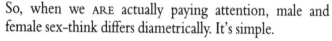

Of course, premature ejaculation means you've only got time to lie back and think of Eng—

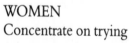

So, when we ARE actually paying attention, male and female sex-think differs diametrically. It's simple.

WOMEN	MEN
Concentrate on trying TO come	Concentrate on trying NOT to come

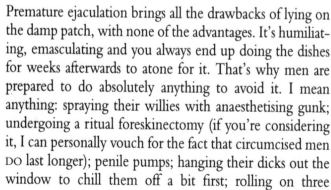

Premature ejaculation brings all the drawbacks of lying on the damp patch, with none of the advantages. It's humiliating, emasculating and you always end up doing the dishes for weeks afterwards to atone for it. That's why men are prepared to do absolutely anything to avoid it. I mean anything: spraying their willies with anaesthetising gunk; undergoing a ritual foreskinectomy (if you're considering it, I can personally vouch for the fact that circumcised men DO last longer); penile pumps; hanging their dicks out the window to chill them off a bit first; rolling on three condoms at once to deaden the immersion experience. If it promises to postpone blast off, you name it, blokes have tried it.

DELAYING TACTICS (A)

Of course, the traditional tried and tested method of prolonging male performance is to force oneself through complicated mental hoops. Most men favour brain-numbing boredom. A mental sprint through the multiplication table – particularly the nine times – mid-bonk is a popular classic. Men with Maths O level tend, rather flashily, to play fast and loose with square roots. Those of sporting bent prefer to plod doggedly through entire Wisdens of cricket scores. I did once jiggle genitals with a chap who admitted to running through Latin conjugations to sustain the heat of the moment, but he was a smug bugger and I should have known better.

DELAYING TACTICS (B)

If boredom isn't your bag, you can always opt for the Tragedy Technique. Think 'Kleenex Factor'. If a thought's not sad enough to soak up at least five, don't waste time thinking it. Grandma's funeral is a hardy perennial. Failing a deceased grandmother, simply use your knowledge of current affairs to commandeer an appropriate horror: inner-city homelessness, acid rain, famine, DIY, drought, Virginia Bottomley. As a quantity surveyor once said: 'I tend to think about Bambi's mother, the food in Tenerife, the size of my mortgage repayments – anything really sobworthy. It sounds sick, but it's amazing how it cools your passion. I reckon it extends my performance by 5–10 minutes. And that can make the difference between a cosy afterglow with After Eights and an icy aftermath vacuuming her Fiesta.'

aWOOooo..!

Naturally, there are occasions when both sexes would benefit from more enthusiasm, not less. That's where Kim Basinger, Alan Titchmarsh and Trevor MacDonald come in. It isn't humanly possible to generate horny, unprintable thoughts about a bloke you've watched pick his toe-nails for the past ten years. Particularly when the most macho thing he's ever done is unbung the sink. Likewise, it's unbelievably tough working up much of a lather over the woman whose Vicks Sinex nasal squirts have punctuated your most tranquil snoozes for a decade and a half. Tender, loving sentiments are all very well on a birthday card, but bugger-all use as erogenous detonators. Those who groan loudest make sure their home thoughts roam abroad.

In yet another excruciatingly expensive, statistically accurate world survey (I asked my Mother's next door neighbour and her niece, my hairdresser, three couples who came to buy my house (but didn't even make an offer), two estate agents, my cousin Bev, my best friend Deborah and five people queueing in front of me at the Kosher butcher), I identified Britain's favourite choice for fantasy fornication in order of preference.

MALE	FEMALE
Princess Diana	Al Pacino
Michelle Pfeiffer	Pavarotti
Betty Boothroyd	Trevor MacDonald (not to
Kim Basinger	be confused with Ronald
Sue Lawley	McDonald)
	Michael Heseltine
	The Chief Rabbi

The moral issue

Are there rights and wrongs in sex-think? Is your beloved more brutally betrayed if you conjure up Jeff Goldblum's goolies, or work out whether your next period's due in the middle of your fortnight in Magaluf? Should we stifle that Keanu Reeves/Jacuzzi/crème caramel fantasy and replace it with decorous domestic musings? Ought we to censor our miscreant minds? Do we owe it to our sweethearts never, ever to picture ourselves sucking on a shared spaghetti strand with Bob Monkhouse? Is bed in the head as bad as bed in the flesh? Frankly, I haven't the foggiest, but at least it gives you something meaty to think about next Friday night.

FRANKLY
UNSUITABLE
FANTASIES

1 Donny Osmond
2 Marie Osmond
3 Jimmy Osmond
4 Rod Hull and Emu
5 Mr Blobby
6 The Tetley Tea Folk

Babies
As
Aphrodisiacs

11

The Sperm's Still Doggy Paddling Up To The Egg - And Already I've Gone Off It

Your Mother was right. The whole point of sex is procreation. You may think you're itching to ride him back and forth like a camel at London Zoo because he's got a biteable bum, tarantula lashes and a metallic silver BMW. Wrong! Lust doesn't come into it. Progesterone does. Face it, we women are martyrs to our hormones. I know it's the sort of thing that male chauvinist swine who fart in the bath, pop the bubbles and inhale proudly, say aloud in public places. Unfortunately, they're absolutely right. If you don't see yourself as a helpless hormonal victim, think menstrually for a moment. Isn't it true that for three weeks of the month you can stroll past a Toblerone without breaking into a sweat, foaming at the mouth, tipping your handbag out on the pavement to scrabble for 2p's and ripping open the wrapper with your teeth? Isn't it true that for three weeks of the month you can watch the Andrex puppy capering about with a mouthful of bog roll without crumpling into hysterical sobs? Isn't it true that for three weeks of the month when your adored one grunts 'morning' as you bump in the bathroom, you can usually bring yourself to grunt 'morning' back? Why do you think it is that on the fourth week, he grunts 'morning' and you jab him in the eye with a toothbrush and scream: 'Don't be so bloody personal!'?

If a mere blip in your lunar cycle criminally corrupts your taste-buds, tear-ducts and temper, how can you deny the obvious? Oestrogen rules OK. And not just at 'that time of the month' either. If we're not menstrual, we're either pre-menstrual or post-menstrual. When we rush out and blow Nat West's two hundred quid on a pair of crushed velvet bell-bottoms we'll never cram our voluminous behinds into, is it because we've got sod all fashion sense and no appreciation of the value of money? No way. Is it because we're inanely succumbing to peer pressure? Nope. It's the hormonal maelstrom, whirling us into profligacy like flecks of female flotsam.

Though we may delude ourselves that we indulge in copulation of our own free will, the facts are different. The rutting instinct stems from our hormonal yen to be fruitful and multiply. You may have whips, manacles and a vigorous dressing down with a feather duster in mind, but your pituitary gland has other ideas entirely. Your brain says: 'Cor! Looks like a rather robust shag!' Your ovaries say: 'We wanna have his children!' This explains why a sprightly tussle in the back of his Opel Manta frequently leads to bridesmaids, six fondue sets and his'n'hers teasmades. This also explains why some time later you suddenly find yourself chucking your contraceptive pills down the loo.

It's not that we want children. We still vividly remember how much we hated children when we were children ourselves. It's not that we suddenly stop hanging out at raves and start soaking up the vibes at Mothercare instead. It's not even that we're possessed by an irrepressible desire to stencil pale pink bunnies with floppy turquoise ears all

over self-assembly MFI chests of drawers. The reproductive urge is simply a conspiracy of hormonal forces we're powerless to resist. One minute you're playing catch with your cap, the next, you're poking holes in the rubber with a fish fork. Why have you become a closet condom-pricker when you loathe anyone under thirty on sight? Why have you started taking your temperature and measuring the density of your vaginal secretions when you'd rather change a tyre than a nappy? Why have you swapped your nifty two seater for a Volvo built like Hyacinth Bucket? Because your hormones have decreed it's Parenthood Time. So parents, whether you like the idea or not, is exactly what you will become.

As soon as a pack of Pampers hangs over the proceedings, lovemaking takes on a whole new dimension. For the first time ever, orgasms are irrelevant. You don't approach sex frivolously any more. Forget slap and tickle. Forget a bit of a laugh. Sex has become something you tackle with the same singlemindedness you'd devote to, say, defrosting the freezer. You go at it conscientiously, earnestly, methodically. There's no flipping about in the Slug and Lettuce position. Perish the proverbial. The aim is to spurt as many sperm as poss in an eggwardly direction. You can't afford to sacrifice a few precious dribbles for the paltry sake of broadening your carnal knowledge. Before you'd spray the stuff anywhere. Down the lav, in the poinsettia, anywhere. Suddenly you're guarding every cubic millilitre like gold-plated, myrrh-encrusted frankincense. Prospective parents are always circumspect with semen. In translation, that means they're stuck in the missionary position.

Once you've taken the decision to beget offspring, you, quite naturally, want to create the optimum conception conditions. It's the reproductive equivalent of digging in half a dozen sacks of putrifying manure before bedding down the dahlias. Of course, these days, we have the additional benefit of modern technology to put the final nails in the coffin of our sex lives.

Modern technology

(A) THE BALLS

Research shows that centrally heated bollocks are less fertile. Apparently, sweaty testicles stew the vim and vigour out of semen. Synthetic Y-fronts inside shrink-wrapped jeans subject the sperm to swampy sauna conditions. By the time ejaculation occurs, those sleepy little blighters haven't got the energy even to attempt front crawl. They just want to be left alone with some Ambre Solaire, a Jeffrey Archer and a Bacardi and Coke on the rocks.

WHAT TO DO

Throw away all radiators and switch immediately from Y-fronts to pure cotton boxer shorts, thus allowing icy breezes/typhoons/hurricanes to circulate freely and refrigerate the said bollocks. Emergency measures include:

1 Applying ice cubes to balls prior to coitus. (This can also be fun, see Sidney Sheldon's *The Other Side of Midnight*, but only worth it if you have resident domestic staff to change the sheets.)
2 Dangling willy out the window prior to coitus – only applicable from September to May. (NOT ADVISABLE IN A BUILT UP AREA.)

(B) CHOOSING THE SEX

Numerous weighty tomes have been sold on the basis that we can influence the sex of our unborn children. Apart from a load of mock-medical bogus hocus-pocus, their argument rest solely on the assumption that it all depends on the acidity v. alkalinity of your vagina.

WHAT TO DO

Stick expensive plain yoghurt/expensive balsamic vinegar up your vaginal canal. Don't know why, but economy own brands are never deemed quite scientific enough. Which for boys and which for girls? Dear God, I don't know. And who cares anyway? A baby is a baby. Some of them can't help being born boys. If you really want to rig the odds that badly, I'd say you deserve a few months leaking yoghurt with knickers you could dip chips into.

(C) SPERM STRENGTHENING

Abstinence makes the heart grow fonder. It also, say the sexperts, makes the sperm last longer. If you want to ejaculate veritable Mark Spitzes, conserve supplies.

WHAT TO DO

Don't.

Once a week, max., with chilly balls, a vagina oozing fromage frais and half an hour afterwards with your legs above your head to do full justice to the forces of gravity – nothing quite like it for cooling one's ardour. 'If we can just get this conception thing over we'll be back in the first flush of lust,' you tell yourselves. OH NO YOU WON'T. The instant that valiant sperm head-butts his way into that welcoming egg, your hormonal turmoil cranks up a gear.

All over the body you thought you knew and loved, lurid, horrible *Jurassic Park* special effects start happening. What sort of things? See next chapter.

P.S. You may have noticed the remarkable popularity of the wedding video. Have you thought what a uniquely charming sharing experience it would be to treat the family, close friends and total strangers to the conception video. Tripods are available from your nearest branch of Dixons. For those on limited budgets, the north-west London Yellow Pages is also excellent.

$\clubsuit$ 12 $\clubsuit$

Sex During Pregnancy (Or, Even With A Pillow Under My Bum I Feel Like A Sodding Book-end)

You can't switch on Oprah Winfrey for five minutes without Elizabeth Taylor discussing her fungal infections or some woman saying: 'Well, I felt a bit funny. I thought it might be the pineapple chunks. So, anyway, I popped into the Ladies and little Kylie-Winona slid out. If the attendant hadn't fished her out, she'd have drowned. Honestly, you could have knocked me down with a feather.' Meanwhile, every other mother in the country is biting furious holes in the three piece suite and screaming: 'WHAT DID YOU SAY? You didn't REALISE you were PREGNANT! I HATE YOU! Lucky bitch!'

Let's get this straight. There are only seven women in the entire universe who go through pregnancy without knowing it. And they've all snapped up mega bucks to talk placentas on Oprah's sofa. Real women know they're pregnant from the moment sperm meets egg. I remember it well. It was 1991; a Saturday; Rickmansworth; a.m.: I was at the zenith of intellectual athleticism, thrusting and parrying my way round Pinner Waitrose, unleashing my finely honed badinage at the condiments and pickles. P.m.:

we repaired for a siesta. Halfway through the afterglow my breasts began to swell. By the time my husband came back upstairs with a cup of Tetleys and a KitKat, I was on my knees before the Armitage Shanks, spitting goodbye to breakfast. I didn't need to pee in that little test-tube thing and wait for the ring to go blue. (Which is fortunate because test-tubes may be fine for men, but I'm not sure womankind is equipped to wee in the sort of single-minded-test-tube-filling trickle essential to stop urine overflowing all over her control top tights.)

And the changes weren't merely physical. From the instant of creation my personality underwent a profound change. It evaporated. In all modesty, unpregnant, I'm a Bolshie, opinionated, dictatorial, in-your-face kinda gal. Pregnant, I'm an insipid, malleable milksop. I put it down to anaemia; or piles; or bleeding gums; or varicose veins of the vulva; or frequency of micturition – getting up sixteen times in the night to pee; or toothache, backache, sinusitis, constipation, sciatica. At my first antenatal appointment – the one where he's supposed to pump your hand and say congratulations – my GP presented me with a special NHS pamphlet called something like: PREGNANCY: TELL THE FACT FROM THE FICTION. Page 1 was a belter.

True or false?

1. Pregnancy makes your teeth fall out.
2. Pregnancy makes your hair (public and pubic) fall out.
3. Pregnancy gives you nosebleeds.
4. Pregnancy means you can't keep anything down for six months except wallpaper paste and Bisto white sauce granules.

5 Pregnancy means you can't leave home without a tupperware bowl in case you have to (a) puke into it (b) wee into it.

6 Pregnancy means both breasts will feel as though they've just gone ten rounds with Lennox Lewis.

Answers

1 True.
2 True.
3 True.
4 True.
5 True.
6 True.

Trendy gynaes claim pregnancy is a 'natural condition, not an illness'. You try telling that to a nouvelle haemorrhoid sufferer with what looks like a bunch of Californian seedless poking out of her bottie.

The blooming myth

Pregnant women are officially supposed to bloom. It says so. Every bloody where: *Middlemarch*, *The Bible*, Mother & Baby magazines, Flora margarine commercials. So, you wait. Your nipples change overnight from pale rose pink to charred toast brown, and still you wait. A dark tidemark bisects your abdomen, giving you all the allure of a equatorial relief map. (Does it mean you're splitting in half? 'Nope', says your GP 'It's the *linea negra*. Happens in 20 per cent of cases.') You curse your genes, become the first woman in history to dab Estée Lauder 'Sahara' Foundation

JOKE

Dr: Mrs Cohen, I've got great news, you're pregnant.
Mrs Cohen: Pregnant? I want a second opinion.
Dr: OK. You're also ugly.

ANTI-JOKE

The Doctor's absolutely right.

all over your belly – and wait. Every morning, you spring
out of bed, vomit all over the patch of carpet you scrubbed
yesterday, hurtle over to the mirror and ask yourself: 'Am
I blooming yet?' Every morning the mirror barks back:
'Sod off, dog-breath!' Total strangers itch to say: 'You're
looking radiant'. Sometimes they actually start to say it
before they realise you most closely resemble the star of a
Pedigree Chum advert. So they peter out mid-gush.
'You're looking r—' 'I'm looking 'r—?' 'Yes. Round. Very
Picasso.'

Believe me, it is medically possible to circumvent the
radiant phase altogether and spend the entire ten months
looking like SHIT. Meanwhile, there is not one particle of
doubt that the only other simultaneously pregnant woman
you know in the whole world will be a whole-hearted
grade A bloomer who drops in after pre-natal yoga classes
and giggles: 'I can't believe I'm still in my jeans at eight
months. Really, I haven't stopped gorging sachertorte and
I've only put on three pounds and my skin's never been
better and my hairdresser Nicky (Clarke, of course) can't
believe how thick and luxuriant my hair is. And *Vogue* has
asked me to sit for Bailey, as Knightsbridge's answer to
Demi Moore. And Rob can't keep his hands off me. And
I'm much more receptive down there. You know, all sort
of moist and welcoming. Even my forehand has improved.
Frankly, I don't want this sprog to be born. I just want to
carry on being pregnant forever.'

She's 'all sort of moist and welcoming' down there.
How are you? Frankly, you've no idea. For all you know,
there's mustard and cress sprouting out of it. For the first
three months He wanted to and you were too busy
nibbling Jacob's Cream Crackers to ward off nausea and
watching your blood dye the green bits pink every time

you bit into an apple to be bothered. For the second three months, you quite fancied it, but He turned out to be the kind of chap who isn't partial to pregnant women because:

a   he's only got the sketchiest grasp of gynaecology and he's worried if he thrusts too hard he'll end up poking the baby in the eye or something.

b   you're about to be a Mother and Mothers aren't supposed to be sexy.

For the third three months he's so knackered stencilling an Etruscan frieze on the nursery ceiling and you're so knackered trying to pull on your pop socks (Ugh! Pop socks! Naff, naffer, naffest! You swore you'd never resort to them, but that was when you were young, naive and could see your feet) that sex is impossible.

Nine months – the pathetic fallacy

Q. How long does human gestation take?
A. Nine months.

No it bloody doesn't. It takes forty weeks. Fours into forty goes ten. That's ten months wearing a 42DD and waddling when you walk. Ten months saying 'Well, I like Sebastian.' 'Well, I don't, it's too poofy.' 'Well, do you like Fabian then?' 'Don't be so moronic.' 'Don't call me a moron, I'm pregnant.' 'I know you're pregnant, you moron. That's why we haven't had sex for nearly a year.' 'OK you brute. If you want sex, we'll have sex.' 'You can't shag something spherical. The underneath areas are too far underneath.' 'You've read Miriam Stoppard. Stick a pillow under your bum.' 'It's YOUR bum you stick it under, you moron. And even with a dozen pillows under it, I still have to lean back so far I feel like a sodding book end.' 'Well, if that's the way you feel about it, what do you think of Zachary?' 'What are you? An imbecile?' 'Don't call me an imbecile, I'm pregnant.'

How do you have great sex during pregnancy?

See Chapter 9, Taking Yourself In Hand.

But don't worry, it can't be long now till those waters break and you get two Reeboks full of amniotic fluid.

❧13❧

Sex With Stitches
(Or, If They'd Sliced Through
Your Willy With A Scalpel, You
Wouldn't Fancy It Either)

Childbirth expert Sheila Kitzinger and her right-on cohorts are desperately keen to have us all sexually entwined right up to the onset of labour. Apparently there's nothing like a fresh spraying of sperm to stimulate your tired old cervix into releasing a barrage of thoroughly fab hormones called prostaglandins. What's more, assiduous nipple tweaking generates another utterly brill hormone called oxytocin. P & O are just what the doctor ordered to launch us into labour with flair and pizzazz. So, it's virtually a moral obligation to keep at it up to and beyond the delivery room door. Sheil would literally adore us to engage in on-the-birthing-stool love-ins, sucking and stroking our way through each contraction while the midwives slip out for a Scotch egg and a couple of Marlboro. As far as I'm concerned, by the time you finally make it into the hospital, you loathe your partner so violently, you'd rather have an internal examination than SHAKE HANDS with the bastard who got you into this mess.

For the last six weeks of pregnancy all sensible women wear Wellingtons and walk very slowly with their legs squeezed tightly together. Why? Because we don't fancy paddling through a medium-sized lake of our own waters, thank you very much. We're working on what my Mother would call: 'The Bursting To Pay A Penny Theory', i.e. if there isn't a loo in sight, clamp your thighs shut, wriggle, avoid dripping taps and willpower will win the day. Unfortunately, what works for wee doesn't apply to amniotic fluid which gushes out of a different place entirely. So when that Niagara Falls falls there's not a darned thing either you or your pelvic floor muscles can do to stop it.

Six rules for breaking waters

Waters only break when:

1   You're in a meeting assuring your boss you're more than able to head up the new account, motherhood isn't going to change a thing.
2   You're sitting on a pale pink brocade chaise-longue in Harrods' Furniture Department, taking the weight off your feet.
3   You're on the 34 bus, and six strange pensioners are pointing at the flood and screaming.
4   You're at the Abbey National, and you're really pissed off because you were trying for Marks & Sparks. (Legend has it that if you go into labour at M & S, you get a free layette.)
5   You're in a crowded cinema, the film is superb, and there's no way of sidling out without soaking the chap next to you's popcorn.
6   You're in the presence of royalty.

Six rules for non-breaking waters

Waters never, ever break when:

1 There's nothing on telly, you've got plastic knickers poised and there's F-all else to do.
2 Your gynae tells you they will.
3 Your Mother tells you they will.
4 Your husband says: 'It would be convenient p.m. on the 17th, between the conference in Brussels and the six day residential seminar.'
5 You've put down an acre of waterproof sheeting, just in case.
6 You didn't like the settee anyway and you can claim it back on the insurance.

Natural childbirth

I'd like to meet the sadist responsible for coining the phrase natural childbirth and give him a natural vasectomy. Something somewhere doesn't add up. Men require linctus, emergency bed-rest, regular infusions of hot whisky and lemon and convalescence in the Seychelles if they nick themselves shaving. Women are compelled to pass the equivalent of the entire *Encylopaedia Britannica* out through our nether regions, and we're made to feel hideously guilty if we ask for so much as an Anadin.

BREATHING: THE DO'S AND DON'TS
You can tell an NCT antenatal class by the slinky Jane Fonda type in an alarming assortment of lycra workout wear who assumes the lotus position and snarls: 'Now then,

after me, huff huff, puff puff, pant pant.' Marooned on the bean bag, what the hell else can you do? 'Huff huff,' you say, with all the enthusiasm you can muster. 'This is not a Shakespeare recitation,' snaps Jane Fonda. 'You'll never make any birthing headway until you appreciate the importance of breathing.' To tell you the truth, I'd never lost much sleep over my breathing prior to antenatals. To be honest, I thought I had breathing pretty neatly sussed. 'How's your breathing?' you might have asked me. 'Piece of cake,' I'd have naively replied. It takes a few sessions with a Natural Childbirth Trust teacher to convince you you've been making a right pig's ear of breathing all along!

It's amazing. Some inebriated maniac dreamed up the inane, insane idea that if you breathe while you're doing it, labour doesn't hurt. Bollocks! Think about it next time you staple your finger to a cheque or drop a frozen turkey on your toe. Presumably you were breathing when the mishap occurred. Did the fact that you were breathing obliterate the pain? Or did you find a dab of witch-hazel, a stiff gin and a handful of Valium a great deal more effective?

YOU CAN TRY THIS AT HOME

Humour me. Stick one forefinger at each corner of your mouth. Pull each corner outwards in the direction of the ear nearest to it. Keep pulling. Then breathe deeply and pant, 'Huff huff, puff puff'. Still hurt? You bet it does. Now try stretching your bottom lip up over your head; breathe 'huff huff, puff puff'. Still hurt? Like stink it does. And believe me, a good swab down with a natural sponge ain't going to make one iota of difference.

THE UNKINDEST CUT OF ALL

In theory, vaginas are elastic. In practice, they're more like sad old knicker elastic than rippling rubber bands. Stretchwise, we have our limitations. Tampons? No probs. Penises? A dab of KY and we'll expand to meet the challenge. A courgette? Sure, why not. A tomato? Rather messy, but what the heck! But a large, juicy, 60p each navel orange? Sorry mate, wrong shape, wrong size. No can bloody do. Logically speaking, if you can't get an orange IN without peeling and segmenting it, it's not going to be *déjeuner sur* frigging *l'herbe*, getting a baby's head OUT. Do they leave us to test our elasticity to its limits? Or brandish the knife and slice? I was going to say obstetricians are torn. But they're not, it's women who might be torn if they let us stretch too far. So rather than risk a tear – which might be jagged and inconvenient to sew up, but which might equally well NOT be jagged or inconvenient to sew up – the powers that are generally opt to cut. The interventionist cut in the perineum is known as an episiotomy. This makes everyone feel better because it sounds medical and necessary. 'A gash through your vagina', might not go down quite so well.

Episiotomies have to be stitched up, which means lying knickerless with your knees in stirrups and a Senior House Officer's head between your legs while the rest of the family pass round cigars, swig your Lucozade, dab their eyes and sob 'I think he's got Grandpa Goldfarb's chin'. Stiched up vaginas, especially bruised, battered vaginas out of which an eight pound hulk has just bashed his way, hurt as if you've posted shards of broken glass up your twat. They'll tell you it's discomfort. Crap. It's unparalleled agony, and when you urinate it's worse.

THINGS YOU
FEEL LIKE
DOING AFTER
AN EPISIOTOMY

1 Sitting astride a
packet of frozen
peas, to
anaesthetise your
stitches.
2 Blowing your
Clairol 200
hairdryer up your
fanny to dry off
your stitches.
3 Sitting on an
inflated child's
rubber ring, to
take the pressure
off your stitches.
4 Chopping a couple
of inches off your
partner's penis.

THINGS YOU
DON'T FEEL LIKE
DOING AFTER AN
EPISIOTOMY

1 Having your labia
pierced.
2 Riding a bicycle.
3 Shouting 'Come
and get me, big
boys!' at the Spurs
football team.
4 Asking a friend to
wax your pubic
hair into an
attractive heart
shape.

★ ★ ★

Doctors have a bizarre habit of asking newly stitched mothers what they intend to do about contraception when they get home. Most of them, suffused with the first rosy glow of parenthood give the only sensible answer: '★★★★ OFF!!, YOU ★★★★★★★ CREEP!'

❀14❀

Sex After Pregnancy (Also Entitled: Sex After Pregnancy - Are You Insane?)

 Re: postnatal sex, there are three important points to remember.

1   After a vaginal delivery your tunnel of love most closely resembles:
    a   the Blackwall Tunnel
    b   the Channel Tunnel
    c   the Cheddar Gorge
2   You could send Take That, Dennis Skinner and a scrotum (official collective noun, I checked) of Chippendales up there all at once and you wouldn't feel a thing.
3   YOU DON'T CARE!!!!!

There are special exercises designed to give you a vaginal facelift. They DON'T involve:

1   lime green leotards with matching footless tights
2   membership of a health club
3   cumbersome items of equipment which clutter up the living room
4   Jane Fonda

5   stepping on and off a milk crate to the tune of 'YMCA'

They DO involve:

1   Contracting your pelvic floor muscles. If you didn't realise your pelvics had a ceiling, let alone a floor, try stopping yourself mid-wee. If you can stop/start/stop/start those golden showers you'll soon be able to shoot pingpong balls out of your doodah and land a holiday job in a Bangkok sex show.

So, we're agreed, you don't have to be Sally Gunnell to get to grips with pelvic floors. Surely anything that transforms your whatsit from a Tesco carrier bag to a tight little Smarties tube is worth having a bash at? But do we bother? Don't be ridiculous. We're far too busy being humiliated by...

Breastfeeding

Looks like the most natural thing in the world doesn't it? *I* thought so: nipple–baby; baby–nipple. Hey presto! Free flowing antibodies. And the bigger the boobs the better. If breast is best, stands to reason jumbo knockers must be double best with brass knobs on. After all Leonardo, Tintoretto and the gang didn't even bother scraping off their palettes for flat-chested Madonnas. Let me tell you something. Babies hate big gazongas. Daddies like them, but babies are absolutely bloody terrified of them. Think about it. Baby's head: size of a Jaffa orange, Mummy's boob: size of a Mitsubishi Shogun. It's no problem if you're an hour-glass figured octopus. You just need one hand to hold the baby, two to wring the nipple into a teat shape, another two to clear an airway between infant nostrils and Mummy's bosom to prevent suffocation and one for nail-biting to ease the tension. I stuck with it, but still cringe at the memory of accosting strange traffic wardens and saying: 'Excuse me, would you mind holding this nipple for a minute while we latch on?'

MAKING A CLEAN BREAST OF IT

Breast feeding is so bizarre, no-one, especially your Mother, has the heart to give you advance warning of the sci-fi nightmare in store. Two days after pushing out the placenta, you're still sitting snugly inside your 36DD. On the third morning, you wake up and something drastically abnormal has occurred. The world has turned pink. You can't see. You can't hear. In pure panic you scream 'Nurse! Help!' but no-one comes near because your mouth is entirely covered by a rock hard, lobster pink object. Working entirely by feel, it takes a couple of hours to deduce that the object is, in fact, a pair of objects, attached to your own chest. Peering over your distended pro-truberances, Nurse, when she arrives, is reassuring. 'Don't worry. It's just your milk coming in.' Don't worry!! Remember space hoppers? Those neon orange rubber bubbles we used to bounce round the garden on? That is what has happened to your tits. Pull down your bra and jets of gold top shoot from your nipples like Quasar lasers and drench the woman-in-the-next-bed's bonsai. Every time you try nourishing your son and heir a fountain squirts out and fills up his left ear. Your mother-in-law rings specially to tell you to scrub your nipples with a nail brush to toughen them up to do their duty. And every time a baby cries on EastEnders you lactate in sympathy and drench your button-through nightie. (N.B. This doesn't matter all that much as there are dollops of infant puke on both shoulders anyway.)

YOUR CUP RUNNETH OVER

The primary problem with being postnatal is ooze. If you're not leaking wetly into your breast pads, you're trickling moistly into your family sized, super absorbent, never-see-these-whoppas-on-the-telly, sanitary towels. Manage to catch a cold from permanently exposing your mammaries to the elements, and you won't have a single ooze-free orifice. Bear this in mind: if you're not dabbing at your own effluent, there's a ceaseless dribble of excrement emanating from both ends of your offspring. You watch, helplessly, as your carefully casual decor is submerged under entire rain forests of Scotties, Kleenex, kitchen roll, J-cloths, muslins, cotton wool balls, Baby Wet Ones and assorted ecologically unsound shit-swabbers.

The shitty gritty

Call me naive (I've been called a lot worse), but most adults I know, with the notable exceptions of:

1 sewage treaters
2 bowel surgeons
3 coprophiliacs (turd-lovers – James Joyce was a rampant afficionado)

don't have all that much to do with shit. Apart from depositing one's own in the nearest convenience, and the odd forcible encounter with the canine variety, one could flourish for decades without eyeballing an alien Number

Two. So much so, in fact, that it becomes almost possible to think of the passing of faeces as a peripheral part of life; an irrelevance; a non-issue; something one absent-mindedly acknowledges by replenishing toilet paper supplies; something one knows exists, like bridge, or Scottish dancing, but refuses to allow to impinge on one's equilibrium. Parenthood changes all that. The very severing of the umbilical cord plunges one into a stinking miasma of wees and poohs. And NO, it IS NOT true that if it's your own child's you actually feel quite attached to it. You don't. You feel like:

a   throwing up all over the appliqued ducks swimming across the nappy stacker
b   pretending you couldn't smell it and leaving it for your partner
c   getting a job – ANY job, organ donor, John Major's caterer – in order to pay someone else to de-turd your kid.

So you've been deluged with booties and cardies and nappies and teddies and absolutely everything that ends in 'ies' except what you really wanted – readies. The place is overflowing with wilting gladioli, antique aunts, plastic Zebedees that go 'boing' and community midwives wanting clean towels. This is where new Mum and new Dad differ for the first time.

Important classified information

NHS gynaes have their patients back in the mish/rabbinical position at six weeks and a day. Go privately, on the other hand, and Harley Street obstetricians, bowing to

🍓 Babies As Aphrodisiacs

MALE THINK

OK, it's born. Jesus, I bought her daffs and a gooey card. How much longer till I get some decent nookie? After all, who was the one wielding the natural sponge, for God's sake?

FEMALE THINK

Sex? Maybe later, when my stitches are out and I'm not so knackered and little Joshua is happily settled – at University.

DR DR

Fortunately medical science comes to the rescue here. Most NHS doctors recommend abstaining until after the six week check up.

behind the scenes pressure from ladies who lunch, but would rather not do anything else, will quietly take husbands aside and whisper the following: 'Old boy, of course, you'll understand the importance of restraint on the marital front. Her 'wedding tackle' needs rehabilitation. So, I'd suggest cold showers and long jogs for six months, minimum.' Having a baby privately costs upwards of two thousand quid – but you do get a better class of baby that way. And, ladies, if it lets you off the conjugal hook for half a year, it may turn out to have been well worth it.

✿ 15 ✿

Mums Don't Come!
(Or, Of Course I Won't Tickle
Your Testicles I'm A Mother!)

Some men like sleeping with Mothers. Some rather fancy their own (see Freud, Sigmund). Some don't mind tinkering with other people's. Most, however, are sexually paralysed by going to sleep married to a woman and waking up married to a MOTHER. When my first child was born, my Father arrived at the Hospital sobbing. 'Dad,' quoth I, 'tears of joy?' 'Nonsense!' he replied tears streaming down his face, 'I've just realised I had carnal knowledge of a GRANDMOTHER last night.'

When you're a parent, sex of all sorts is chronically lacking in decorum. Most of us can't remember our own Mothers chomping on the paternal earlobes during Mrs Dale's Diary, so we resist any urge to practise such a recondite perversion ourselves. Furthermore, most of us can't recall our own Fathers whipping off their braces and anchoring Mum to the Aga for an all-tongues snogging session. Being parents and horny as hell isn't nice. It's not decent to harbour rubber/bondage fantasies about the mother/father of your children. Anyway, lust is reserved for bad girls and boys. Do you think Sly Stallone was a Johnson's Baby? Can you seriously see Rambo, powder puff poised over infant bot? And what about Madonna?

JOKE

Child pyschologist: **Mr and Mrs Cohen, I don't know how to break this terrible news to you. Your son, Irving has the worst Oedipus complex I've seen in forty years as a practitioner.**
Mrs Cohen: 'Oedipus, SchmOedipus, what does it matter as long as he loves his Mother?'

87

Picture those Gaultier conical cod pieces patterned with fresh baby up-chuck and pureed potato. When sex symbols do sully their image by procreating, most have the good sense to keep their children thousands of miles outside paparazzi zoom lens range. Boarding school up an unassailable Alp in tax free Switzerland is a favourite film-star 'Children? Me? Well, not as such' dodge.

My neighbour, now an eminently respectable mother of three, was famous for frolicking about her bachelor flat in her pre-PTA days, exuberantly starkers. 'I was at ease with my body and at ease with my randyness,' she blurted. (After six or seven Um-Bongos, she becomes either maudlin or expansive.) 'It was OK to love sex. There's one particularly energetic episode on the doormat I feel especially nostalgic about. These days I wouldn't dream of letting it all hang out. Admittedly, there's a lot more of it to hang. I keep my bathrobe by the bed. Since the kids, I suppose the best word for our sex-life is discreet: no loud bangs, no animal groans. Somehow anything more flamboyant doesn't seem quite cricket.'

What's worse, your genitals don't feel like your own anymore.

Males

That trusty pork sword you used to poke merrily into the most sordid nooks and crannies has suddenly acquired social status as a baby planter. Flesh of your flesh has sprung, wailing, from seed of your seed. Your penis is every inch a phallic fertility symbol. Can you grab your son's point of origin cavalierly during Baywatch and manhandle it to the point of no return? Of course you can't. Yesterday's winkle was there for the jerking. Today's is hallowed, paternal, publicly acclaimed. When strangers coo: 'Bootiful baby,' you know they're really saying: 'Your Dad certainly had a fine, upstanding, fully functioning penis to sire a bonny fellow like you, Sonny.' Your relationship with your penis has changed beyond recognition. Before you were chums, mates, partners in . . . well, in anyone you could get into, really. Now you treat each other with respect. In the bath, you lather on the Camay, with awe. Blessed are the son-makers.

Female

It's not that you felt all that enthusiastic about your vagina in the first place. The truth is, you always thought it looked like a suppurating limb stump, smelled distinctly kipperish and had a periodic tendency towards unpleasant secretions. Nevertheless, it was a foul thing, but thine own. What's more, it gripped like a limpet. You were known through-out the Borough of Barnet as a tight squeeze. Now your parts have been stretched to the size of a prize-winning watermelon, sliced through and stitched up in a strange freehand embroidery style by an exhausted junior doctor. What's more, they're hardly private. You're most intimate undulations have been ogled, tweaked and prodded by more midwives, consultants, rubber gloved medical stu-dents, Filippino floor cleaners and mis-routed visitors, who actually wanted the ENT ward on the third floor, than you care to remember. In fact, at one point, you dimly remember offering to distribute Cornettos to the first fifteen rows of spectators. (I blame Virginia Bottomley. At my local GP's, they're so cost-conscious, the cleaning lady

ACCEPTABLE
BEHAVIOUR
POST-
PARENTHOOD

taking out a school fee
   insurance policy
buying a family dog
joining a golf club
cutting the coupons
   off Pampers'
   packets
breast feeding
hand knits
baby talk
making a will

does the coil fitting. Apparently, they did a time and
motion study – and she was the one already wearing the
rubber gloves.) Frankly, it's not the organ you knew. Your
vagina has emerged with dignity, a veteran, bruised and
battered yet unbowed. Subjecting it to the frivolous
onslaught of mere sexual intercourse is unthinkable.
Awarding it the George Cross? Perhaps. Mounting it on a
plinth and exhibiting it at the V & A? Possibly. Writing a
florid history of its hard won battle scars for *The Sunday
Times*? Certainly. Engaging in run of the mill, common or
garden rumpy-pumpy? Unthinkable.

As for your boobs? Desmond Morris in *The Naked Ape*
may blather all he likes about big tits being nothing to do
with maternity and everything to do with sexuality.
Apparently apes have no bosoms at all – just cigar-length
nipples – and they do a spiffing job of breastfeeding.
'Boobs,' says Des, 'serve no biological function. They're
buttock-mirroring sex toys.' Try telling that to someone
with one cracked nipple, one caught in the zipper of her
feeding bra, a blocked milk duct, mastitis, cabbage leaves
on her cleavage to bring down the swelling and nine
pounds of squalling infant en route to malnutrition.
Breastfeeding bosoms may be sexy to babies, daddies,
gawpers and gropers. Rest assured they are only slightly less
sexy than projectile vomiting to their owners.

What to say if he initiates sex

'No.'
   'I said, "No".'
   'Are you deaf as well as stupid. When I say sodding no.
I mean sodding no.'

'Bugger off, you sex-crazed swine.'

'Oh, all right then. But only if you unload the washing machine, hoover the lounge, make me a nice cup of tea and do the nine o'clock feed first.'

He: 'How can I do the nine o'clock feed, you're breast feeding, for Christ's sake?'

She: 'If you loved me, you'd find a way.'

What to say if she initiates sex

Depending on your mood, choose either:

a   You've got it wrong, Sweetheart. It isn't my birthday till NEXT Tuesday.

or

b   'Don't blow on my testicles. I'm a Father.'

What to say if anyone mentions sex

'Sssh! Not in front of the baby.'

What to do if anyone on television has sex

Switch off immediately and watch the home video of your natural childbirth all over again. If those ovarian close-ups don't put sex in its proper perspective, the petri dish overflowing with placenta definitely will.

But all is not lost. Some time before your child's first birthday (only hours before in my case), your hormones will start flinging out the occasional sex-driven signal.

You'll be amazed to discover yourselves mildly drawn towards a spot of groin grinding. 'My God, I want you!' you pant hungrily, ripping off layers of one another's clothing. 'My God, I'm going to show you the shag of the century,' you breathe, lunging for the chandelier. His helmet makes its first blissful inroad into your unplumbed depths, after months of celibacy, you're finally floating on a supersonic surfboard built for two. And it feels soooo gooood. I said, soooo gooood. I said, sooooo—, when CRASH! £££! You thrill to the expensive sound of cost-the-earth Wedgwood dinner-service fracturing against arm-and-a-leg champagne flutes as chuckling crawler deliberately head-butts wall unit – coitus thoroughly and irrevocably interruptus.

Your hormones have let you down again. If you thought sex with a baby in the house was a bad joke, things can only get worse. If you can face it, pour something stiff and rockless and see next chapter.

Toddlers
As
Aphrodisiacs

☙ 16 ☙

Dad Gets An Erection.
Junior Gets An Ear Infection

Toddlers are like dolphins only far less diverting conversationalists. Both species are slimy and both come equipped with immensely sophisticated and sensitive radar. I loathe nature, and something American with Jane Seymour and sequinned shoulder pads always seems to be on at the same time as David Attenborough, so I confess to not having the remotest inkling what dolphin radar are for. Although, now you mention it, I do seem to remember Flipper – Flipper, faster than lightning – tracking down a weekly supply of murderers and miscreants with his (hers?) (Or was that Skippy, the bush kangaroo?) Anyway, I know exactly why toddlers need radar. They use it, like sad old Squidgygate mobile phone hams, to pick up on the first delicately tentative shoots of renaissance in parental sexuality. Having detected a paternal pat on the maternal behind, or a matriarchal snuggle against a patriarchal shoulder, toddlers are merciless. They will stop at nothing in their mission to exterminate your sex-life. If kiboshing your bonking prospects involves contracting chicken-pox or rolling off their changing mats and becoming violently impaled on a nappy pin, they will do so unflinchingly. If they deem it necessary to impede your amours, they will fluctuate remorselessly between diarrhoea and constipation for months at a stretch. They also excel at something called 'making him/herself sick'. This physiological phenomenon never takes place during daylight hours. However, the faintest rustle of a condom wrapper, or the distant slurp of spermicide on cap, is the only catalyst necessary to ensure Junior, babygro, cot bumper, your dressing gown and the entire stuffed menagerie are doused from stem to stern in regurgitated broccoli. Who's waving 'bye bye' to the nice Big O, then?

Top ten toddler tricks to stop play

1 Remove dummy from mouth. Fling on floor. Howl like spayed cat until parent retrieves and plugs in.
2 Repeat 1.
3 Repeat 2.
4 Stick a piece of Lego up your nose.
5 Hurl yourself headlong over the bars of your cot, crawl, past ungated stairs, at colossal personal cost to life and limb, along corridor to parents' room and say 'Boo!'
6 Perfect a sound that might, conceivably, be whooping cough. Repeat sound at sixty second intervals all night. Fall into a satisfied sleep just as GP arrives.
7 Evacuate a pooh from Hell. Make sure to smear it up your back, down to your knees, and cake clods of it in your hair. Leave the question of whether or not you've eaten any delightfully enigmatic.
8 If you are demand fed, demand a feed. If you are not, demand one anyway. Deliberately withhold the post prandial burp. Then shriek inconsolably. They'll put it down to 'wind'.

9 Get the hang of pulling the string on the horrible tinny musical box that plays 'Twinkle frigging twinkle'. Hook your toe round it and continue pulling, even while technically asleep.

10 When your Father takes said music box and jumps on it fifty-seven times while foaming at the mouth, you can congratulate yourself on a sex-life well and truly scuppered.

N.B. Those are only the Top 10 ways, favoured by the conformist, clichéd toddler.

More idiosyncratic methodology flourishes among dis-affected toddlers who refuse, on principle, to read Pen-elope Leach. This includes:

1 Breath holding. Most effective if you refrain from inhaling until you turn purple as bortsch.

2 Head banging. Make sure the item you select to batter with your skull is a) of immense sentimental value and b) irreplacable.

3 Masturbating in public places. No good in a p.c. environment where adults will nod approvingly (and in some cases join in).

4 Being allergic to a) cows' milk b) soya milk c) coconut milk – preferably all three.

5 Starting to read, in several languages, at eighteen months. They will be so busy nurturing your genius by declaiming Virgil in the vernacular, they'll never have a second to consummate.

PARENTALLY
APPROVED
TRANSITIONAL
OBJECTS

- teddies
- bunnies
- pretty little cot
  blankets sprinkled
  with gambolling
  lambs
- dummies
  (orthodontic)
- crocheted shawls
- silk ribbons

Job's comforters

Peace-deprived parents can't wait to take off the heat and fixate their kid on a 'transitional object'. Unfortunately the objects a thirty-five year old adult with a degree in civil engineering deems suitable for fixation rarely coincide with those selected by an eleven-month-old toddler with qualifications in chewing-up tissues and spitting.

Fact

Once fixated, children remain fixated. They are not susceptible to enticing swaps.

Parent: 'Listen, Darling, you give me the stinky old sock and I'll give you five Nintendos, my Bob Dylan collection and a brand new Alfa Romeo on your seventeenth birthday.'

Toddler: 'Nnngh!'

Translation: 'Piss off!'

Fact

The optimum condition for comforters is UNWASHED. Otherwise they don't 'smell right'. 'Right' generally means a purulent stench of rhubarb crumble, congealed carrot, feet, snot, wet beds and generations of Calpol. If you dare purloin the beloved object and subject it to the twin assaults of Daz and Biotex, you will be rewarded by weeks of Chinese Sleep Torture while your child waits, wide awake, for the return of that reassuring sewage scent.

Fact

Your child will insist on carting his comforter everywhere. This means you have ample hourly opportunity to lose it – and ruin his life.

Favourite places for mislaying your child's emotional fulcrum

- Lanzarote Airport
- B & Q
- hard shoulder, M6
- the beach: 'Where?' 'Somewhere near the sea, I think'.
- Harrods' Sale
- Wales

What to do

Rush round dementedly yelling: 'Have you seen a pair of Y-fronts with apple juice stains and melted chocolate buttons on?' at perfect strangers. Don't forget to scream: 'Thanks a lot for helping out you blind old tosspot!' at people who don't immediately put down their iced Daquiris and join the hunt. Should a member of the public approach, cautiously holding your child's pride and joy in a pair of tongs, be sure to grab it and charge off shrieking: 'Noo-Noo! Thank God you've come back! Son, look, Daddy's found Noo-Noo!'

TODDLER APPROVED TRANSITIONAL OBJECTS

- revolting item of dubious origin discarded by neighbouring dog
- rancid dish cloth
- mildewed gardening glove – legacy of posthumous incumbent of your house
- depressing pair of frayed Y-fronts belonging to Father
- ancient pair of Mother's knickers, long since relegated to duster status
- entire bed-sized duvet
- large boxed set of the seven dwarfs

Toddlers As Aphrodisiacs

Stop press

Children never choose socially acceptable names for their comforters. The cachet of 'Caroline' or 'Henry' escapes them. They opt instead for reduplicated monosyllables of the type that will never fail to make you feel a prat-faced twerp everytime you have to utter them in public. (It goes without saying, that you will utter them in public several times a day for the next ten years.) Current favourites in NW10 are at the time of writing are: 'Nyongy-Nyongy', 'Loy-Loy', 'Mu-Mu', 'Ree-Ree', 'Jay-Jay', 'Bim-Bom' and 'Shlushy-Shlushy'. It is as well to practise saying: 'Excuse me, Waiter, could we please have some extra jam for Loy-Loy,' in the privacy of a locked bathroom.

Drugs

You swore you'd never do it, but it's either you or the kid. Parents of all persuasions inevitably end up on their knees, begging the GP for 'a bottle of something to make him sleep. Doctor'. Your GP will refuse. You will then start plucking out handfuls of your hair, barking like a dog and stabbing yourself, repeatedly, with a pair of tweezers. He will eventually realise that when you say 'overwrought', you mean 'overwrought'. He will finally hand over a bottle of Phenergan or Valergan with strict instructions not to exceed the stipulated dose of three drops or an eighth of a teaspoonful. You dash home, take a soup ladle, fill it and dunk Junior's head in it. You sit back and wait for snores. You don't get them.

WHY?

Because yours is the one child in 150 who 'reacts badly' to juvenile soporifics. Other infants subside into a stupor and wake up, well-rested, a week on Friday. Yours takes a swig and roars into turbo-charged, fuel injected dervishdom.

THE ALTERNATIVE

Take a few slugs of Valergan and Phenergan yourself. Junior may be pillaging the umbrella plant, but you'll be too knackered to care.

☙ 17 ☙

Naming Of Parts

'To-day we have naming of parts. Yesterday,
We had daily cleaning. And to-morrow morning,
We shall have what to do after firing. But to-day,
To-day we have naming of parts.'

Henry Reed

A few weeks ago, I faxed an article entitled 'Orgasmic Etiquette' to Mrs Middle-America's favourite browse, *Redbook* magazine. (They pay a dollar a word. Writing 'and' has never been such a turn-on.) My New York editor rang back, fresh from a power-brunch, but puzzled. 'Vanessa,' she said, 'we have a problem we'd like to run by you. We've looked it up in all our dictionaries, but it isn't listed. Can you clarify please, what exactly is a winkle?' 'A winkle?' I replied, transatlantically. 'Well, it's a willie.' Total silence. 'You know, a man's thingie.' Total and extremely expensive silence. 'A John Thomas if you like.' The dime finally dropped. 'You don't mean a penis? Sonofabitch. Why the f★★★ didn't ya say so?'

I didn't say so because I was brought up never to be accurate when a euphemism would do. Chez Feltz, Daddy had a winkle, Mummy had a noonie and we all had bottoms at the back. I'm used to winkle. It's an affectionate, familiar, suck-it-and-see kind of name. Like willie, it's the sort of word you can feel relaxed about. Shorten them to winks, wills, winkie or just 'W' and pretty much everyone in the United Kingdom will get the hang, sorry, drift. Don't you think penises and vaginas sound terribly official? Desperately formal, like something you'd revise for Biology O level. Off

the record, I'd no more call my noonie a vagina than my guts
intestines, or my throat an epiglottis.

'Enough.' I hear you cry. 'I'm a computer programmer.
I couldn't care less WHAT you call it.' You're right, YOU
couldn't. But every minor in the universe is passionately
interested. Granted, you may not make a habit of discussing
your testicles. Gynaecologists (and books like this) apart, I
don't make a habit of discussing my vagina, either.
Children, on the other hand, like nothing better than a
nice long chat about winkles, noonies and bottoms,
preferably in a public place with a selection of vicars,
Chelsea pensioners, the Queen Mother and the Chief
Rabbi well within earshot. My daughters are eight and five
and their phrase-of-choice at the moment is 'two buttocks
make one bum'. Their favourite song is: 'Jingle bells,
Batman smells, Robin's gone away. Uncle Billy lost his
willy on the motorway.' And if they can spice up mealtimes
with a few dozen graphic references to poo-poo and wee-
wee so much the tastier. I'm reassured by been-there-
done-that friends that I ain't heard nothing yet. 'You'd
better resign yourself. They find all this bottom business
screamingly funny for years. It only peters out a few hours
before we start paying out for the wedding flowers,' said
one veteran paterfamilias, wearily.

In an ideal world, children would be obscene and not
heard. In this one, they find nothing more side-splittingly
hilarious than an audience-based genitally focused chat.
How does one cope? Ignore the whole issue? At our peril.
Willies in particular don't take kindly to being ignored.
They're forever bobbing up and down, spraying the carpet,
getting sore or caught in zippers. They're just as visible and
far more fascinating than hands and feet – particularly to
their owners. Face it, if you don't play Name That Organ,

someone else will! My pal Jackie couldn't countenance 'penis' and wasn't prepared to bowdlerise with 'winkle' or, God forbid, 'willie'. So she shut her son's you- know-what firmly away in his nappy and talked about politics and religion instead. So far, so fine, until he came back from nursery school, pulled down his dungarees and announced: 'I've got a tickly feeling in my whanger.' Collapse of gob-smacked censor.

Waiting till children reach playground age is risky. Once they've adopted a juicy nugget like 'arsehole' not even vulgar amounts of cash will wean them off it. Far better to pre-empt matters by allocating them names you can just about tolerate while conscious. (Although I did once consort with a twenty-nine-year-old commodities broker who still called it his 'little man' which was accurate length-wise and something of a passion killer.) Attempting to abolish the snigger factor altogether is futile. After all, giggling about bottoms is one of the primary pleasures of adulthood, not to mention childhood. What you can attempt is to remove the sleaze factor. I'm not at all in favour of my children thinking their private parts are intrinsically dirtier or nastier than their public parts. Everybody has orifices. So I'd rather answer blush-making questions like: 'When will I get a hairy pecker like Daddy's?' in the middle of a crowded dentist's waiting room, than come over all cloak and dagger. Secrecy breeds sleaze, ignorance and embarrassment.

WHAT'S THAT?

Rude bits are funny, and exciting and endlessly interesting. Look at Paul Raymond's bank balance if you don't believe me. Let's face it, we're supposed to be enthralled by them. If we weren't we'd be extinct. So, the bottom line on babies and bottoms is keep your cool, stay unruffled and tell the truth.

This is purely personal, but I detest the idea of calling a vagina 'front bottom'. Firstly it's untrue and confusing. Bottoms are pooh producers, vaginas certainly aren't. Secondly, it deprives little girls of something to call their own. It isn't fair. Boys have willies. Girls are entitled to have sexual organs with an individual identity and title. I'm not berserk about 'vagina', it's a touch clinical, but even that is better than the dreaded 'front bottom'. If you're imaginatively famished, you're welcome to use 'noonie'. Really, think of it as my gift to you. 'Noon' for short. Lord knows where it derives. Probably from a pre-historic Yiddish expletive, but it's always served my clan admirably. An exhaustive survey among my chums shows some call their's 'twinkle' or 'twinx' and a few favour 'fanny' or 'fan'. I even know of one little girl who calls hers 'flower' and you can't say much fairer or sweeter than that.

Of course, toilet talk is an integral penance of bringing forth progeny. Toddlers are so entranced by the contents of their disposables, they literally can't wait to bring them up in conversation. Against all the odds, my elder daughter's first *mot* wasn't 'Dada' but 'poo-poo'. Surprisingly, the penis and vagina contingent, who can't bear the use of anatomical cop-outs, happily compromise their principles where matters lavatorial are concerned. There must be parents who call the stuff 'faeces' and 'excrement', but I've never met them.

Be warned! The boundaries between acceptable bodily function badinage and crudities guaranteed to raise grand-parental eyebrows are frighteningly fuzzy. 'Need a crap, Grandma,' said Joshua down the road. Grandma re-wrote her Last Will and Testament on the spot. Our local headmistress asked a junior mixed infant where he was headed. 'I'm off to take a dump,' came the riposte. If you're seeking inspiration, 'Number 1' for urinating and 'Number 2' for, well, Number 2s, are tried and tested. 'Big jobs' or 'biggies' always sounded unhealthily constipated to me. Call me anally retentive, but I'm a traditionalist. Conservative with the smallest possible 'c', nothing beats good old 'wee-wee' and 'poo-poo' for sheer dependability. Although forty-eight-year-old barristers who 'Hope you don't mind if I stop off here for a poo-poo,' should automatically be disqualified from romantic entanglements.

If you're happiest calling a spade a spade, 'penis', 'vagina' and 'mammaries' are the perfect words for you. If, however, you'd be altogether happier calling it 'the gardener's oojamaflip', do just that. The great thing is to christen your bits. Flunk it and your offspring will grow up to address their most intimate parts in the style of witless misspelled graffiti scrawled on walls in urine-puddled toilets with empty loo rolls. Romeo was talking through his soliloquy when he burbled: 'What's in a name? that which we call a rose By any other name would smell as sweet.' Ask any adult female if she'd rather have a c★★t, a twat, a snatch, a pussy, a vagina, or an unfurled gardenia – and she'll probably punch you in the kisser.

ᯤ18ᯤ

Teenagers Are Worse!
(Or, 'Ugh, You Wrinklies Don't,
Like, You Know, Like, Bonk,
These Days? You Do? Yeeuch!
Gross!')

'Hope I die before I get old!' bawled Roger Daltrey a few generations before mine. He hasn't. Though most teenagers would disagree. To the pubescent anything over thirty IS dead. Sure, it's still good for hot meals, clean laundry, squash racquets, private saxophone lessons, ferrying to and from snoggathons and colouring in the seas in Geography projects, but it's still to all intents and purposes in advanced rigor mortis. Collar a stray teenager and bellow: 'Are your parents human?' and the result will be as follows:

1 Teenager looks blank. Closer inspection reveals Walkman plugs surgically implanted in ears.
2 Teenager shouts 'Can't hear you, mate!' and turns away.
3 Rip plugs from teenager's ears.
4 Give teenager a few minutes to adjust to life at normal decibel level.
5 Repeat the question.

6 Await answer.

7 Continue waiting while teenager guffaws hysterically, slaps thighs, rolls round carpet in paroxysms and splits sides.

8 Teenager assumes expression of the utmost contempt and snorts: 'Them? Human? They listen to Radio 2!'

The key to successful teenhood is twofold:

1 The unshakable conviction that your parents are hopelessly, terminally and untreatably cretinous. Comments like: 'Christ, Dad, everyone knows Snot Smegma hasn't played keyboards with Pus And The Lepers since the Septic Hernia Tour,' and 'Oh my God, those guys over there are in my class. Quick, I'm begging you. I'll do anything. Even accountancy. If you'll put this bag over your head, cross over the road and pretend you're not with me,' are compulsory.

2 The unswerving knowledge that you, personally, invented sex. In rare rational moments, teenagers will reluctantly admit their parents must have had sex, but they are certain a) that was a very, very, long time ago when people still drew funny looking cows on cave walls b) they weren't any good at it.

The idea of OLD people rubbing rude bits brings them out in spots. Though it can be hard to tell as they're out in spots already. Their definition of OLD is:

1 anyone without zits
2 anyone with combed hair
3 anyone who rises during daylight hours
4 anyone who eats meat/fruit/vegetables
5 anyone who thinks Björk plays tennis

Teenagers are selfless in their mission to save you from the embarrassment of attempting sexual congress at your stage of senile decrepitude. There are no lengths to which they are unprepared to resort, in order to save you from undignified mortification of the flesh.

These altruistic manoeuvres include: Bursting into your bedroom at 3.45 a.m. and saying:

a   'That T-shirt. You know. The one I left in the middle of the hall under those pizza wrappers with my football boots and a couple of joss sticks and Graham's jock-strap on top of it. Yeah, the one with the cigarette burns and the ink stains and a dirty great rip on one shoulder.' 'You did WHAT??' 'Threw it away??!' 'How could you? That was my best T-shirt.'

b   'Does my breath smell?' 'Tell me the truth.' 'Dad, wake up.' 'Is Mum lying to me?' 'Does my breath stink?' 'What do I need to know at 3.45 a.m. for?' 'Look, you wouldn't understand. I just need to know. OK?'

c   'Six pounds fifty to pay for Jake's mini-cab.'

d   'Sixteen pounds fifty to pay for Jed's mini-cab.'

e   'Who was Lord Shaftesbury/Pythagorus/Lars Porsena of Clusium?' 'Of course it can't wait. I've got the A level in the morning.'

f   'How hot is the microwave?'

g   'Can I borrow one of Dad's condoms? Just joking!'

h   'Everyone hates me.' Cue for both parents to wake up, assure teenager everyone adores him/her, bring tea and biscuits up on a tray, and lie awake for the next six months saying: 'Our child is unpopular. Where did we go wrong? Well, I'll tell you something. She/He didn't get it from MY side of the family. Your Mother's

TOP TEN WAYS TO
MAKE SURE YOUR
TEENAGER
REMAINS A
VIRGIN

1 Draw it a map of its G-spot.
2 Offer it use of the parental bed for defloration purposes.
3 Repeatedly insist: 'Darling, my contraceptives are your contraceptives.'
4 Buy it a waterbed for Christmas.
5 Have mirrored tiles put on its bedroom ceiling.
6 Don't start breakfast without asking: 'Any good wet dreams lately?'
7 Regularly announce: 'If there's anything you want to know about oral sex, Sweetheart, your Dad and I are here for you.'
8 Say concernedly: 'Your Dad and I would be so disappointed in you if you weren't getting your end away regularly.'

famous the length and breadth of Golders Green for being socially maladjusted. Do you think anyone will ever marry him/her?' while the teenager snores contentedly.

i 'I'm converting to Catholicism.' (If Mum and Dad are Jewish)
j 'I'm converting to Judaism.' (If Mum and Dad are Catholic.)
k 'Can Jem leave his grass-snake in the bath?'
l 'I can't sleep.'

A second highly successful teenage ploy to stymie your sex-life forever is professionally known as 'The Charging Into The Bathroom Gambit'. Experienced practitioners will confirm that this involves charging into a bathroom in which a parent is bathing. Since most parents bathe in the nude, this affords the teenager the ultimate opportunity to scrutinise the bod that bore it and exclaim:

To a mother

*   'Blimey! They've gone all saggy.'
*   'Why are your nipples so knobbly?'
*   'God, that Caesarean scar looks really gross.'
*   'Have you learned to live with your cellulite?'

To a father

*   'Why are your bollocks all droopy?'
*   'Do you ever get used to old age?'
*   'How do you find it under that beer belly?'
*   'Didn't you have biceps once?'

To either

- 'Aren't those liver spots?'
- 'You could always join a gym.'
- 'When do you think the rot set in?'
- 'I didn't realise pubes went grey.'

9 Exclaim: 'GCSEs? Pah! All your Mother and I care about is your track record for cunnilingus.'

10 Explain: 'We know you have the potential to be truly promiscuous. We only hope you won't let the family down.'

The aim is to make you feel so repulsively decayed, you lose no time trading in your Durex Featherlite for a pair of secateurs and a challenging jigsaw puzzle. They want to force you into voluntary sexual redundancy because there's absolutely no point having teenage sex unless it's part of your mainstream rebellion. Shagging goes alongside drink, drugs, installing a nose-ring, painting your bedroom black, changing your name to 'Maggot', failing your GCSEs and jumping off buses without paying, on The List Of Things Parents Most Don't Want You To Do. It's no fun otherwise. It's tough to find sex sinful if you know Mum and Dad are doing it. So making sure they're so busy scooping you off floors and out of police vans they haven't got the energy is an important part of growing up.

Attention all parents. Do NOT accept this onslaught passively. Fight like with like. Refuse point blank to be rebelled AGAINST. The best way to scupper your teenager's sex-life – probably permanently – is to muscle in all smiles, helpful advice and APPROVAL. This is popularly known as taking the wind out of their tails.

Relax. By the time they're thirty-six or thereabouts, they'll have left the nest. There you'll be, starring in your very own sexual idyll. Just you two. Alone and unspied on. Free to live out the rest of your lives without again coming face to face with an alfalfa sprout. Free to remark inno-cently: 'Tofu? Have you seen her in concert?' without having to live it down. Free to iron creases in your jeans. Free to say: 'You've got to hand it to Bruce Forsyth,' without detonating a nuclear attack. Free, moreover, to swing from the strip lighting in nothing but a smattering of Thousand Island should you so desire.

There's just one minor problem. You don't desire. After decades of wishing the children would bugger off to Gretna Green/Willesden Green/pastures green(er) and leave you to get down on it, they have and all you can think of is phoning them urgently to find out whether or not they're wearing a vest/condom?

Smalls Talk

🍓 19 🍓

You Can Tell The State Of A Marriage By The Knickers Rotating On The Washing Line

OK, I admit, I have a vested interest in lingerie. Indeed, having a father known as 'Norman, the Knicker King', my view of vests is more informed than most. I was brought up in knickers. My father travelled in ladies' underwear. Gussets were, quite literally, meat and drink to us. Others split the atom. Dad split crotches. Others sought the holy grail. Dad stalked the earth in pursuit of the perfect pyjama. Countless au pairs fled sobbing, back to Bilbao, after Dad swooped on their smalls saying: 'Just as I thought! Polyester. Made in Mauritius.' He assured me Shakespeare only had it half right with 'The apparel oft proclaims the man'. According to my Dad, the Bard should have put: 'The INTIMATE apparel'.

Underwear: its condition, provenance, pedigree, and history, is the only reliable key to the human psyche. Don't be deluded by Jaeger co-ordinates. Show me a tweed skirt, twin-set and pearls and I guarantee there's a scarlet satin bustier pulsating beneath. The clothes we select for public consumption have bugger all to do with the real us. Buying a Jasper Conran jacket says everything about our response

to the fashion pundits who direct their prayers to 'Armani, which art in Heaven'. Not to mention media pressure, peer pressure, status pressure and Jasper's marketing strategy. It says not a jot about us. Outerwear is compromise and conformity. Underwear – unless you grab your thrills standing, legs splayed, over occupied manholes – is for an invited audience only. Knicker-wise, thank God, we can relax. That's why it goes against the groin to wear power panties. Under many an £800 YSL suit, pairs of BhS 'three for £1.99' panties are flourishing. Proof positive that, when you get to the bottom of things, you can take the girl out of the chain store, but you can never take the chain store out of the girl.

If you want to suss out the state of a relationship don't waste time traipsing off to therapy. Just pop outside and make friends with the washing line.

Good signs (female)

- black bikini briefs
- ivory silk cami-knickers
- matching teddy
- ecru satin body
- Wonderbra

Good signs (male)

- boxers with subtle impressionist pattern
- crisp, white Ys
- high in the thigh black briefs

These demonstrate:

1   a refined aesthetic sense
2   a highly developed hygienic sense
3   self respect. Crummy old knicks are the equivalent of dirt behind the ears, or apple cores behind the radiator
4   respect for your partner's refined aesthetic sense
5   a healthy desire to be fruity

AND THERE'S A HUGE PLUS. If you get killed in a road traffic accident, you won't have to die of embarrassment when the men at the morgue eyeball your smalls.

QUESTION: What if your smalls are BIG?

Bad signs (female)

*   six pairs of identical nylon knicks, all dyed washing machine grey
*   three grotty bras, one with safety pin in strap, one with two bent hooks, one with half the underwiring missing

Bad signs (male)

*   baggy vests with tiny airvent holes all over them
*   Y-fronts with suspicious yellow patches
*   gimmicky boxers with little Xmas puddings on
*   thermal long johns

These demonstrate:

1   you don't give a proverbial
2   you don't give a proverbial if your partner knows you

don't give a proverbial

EVEN WORSE

3   you don't give a proverbial if the NEIGHBOURS know you don't give a proverbial
4   face it, if your knickers are past their sell by date, your sex-life is likewise

'Now, steady on!' I hear you cry. 'There is a recession going on, you know. Some of us have more important things to spend our money on than fancy anus decor.' Granted, on the surface it might appear that a leaky roof/aching tooth is marginally more deserving of investment than oyster crêpe de Chine Directoires. But aren't you thinking rather short-term here? Take a paracetamol, stick a bucket under the deluge and flaunt those frillies. As every cordon bleu knows, presentation is all. If you don't immerse your part in something smart, someone else might.

Could be good/could be bad (both sexes)

- black rubber G-strings
- peekaboo bras with marabou trim
- split crotch leather panties
- pvc corsets with metal studs
- velcro nipple rosettes
- stick on rubies for the navel

All this X-rated mail-order mayhem could be brill/bad news. It might mean:

1   You're a couple of ardent underworld enthusiasts, constantly toddling off to Anne Summers parties and ringing each other at the office for mutual lingerie-

based titillation sessions. 'Hello Sweetcakes, hubbie here. Is it the latex merry widow plunge with nipple zippers? Or the purple lace button-through with extra lycra today?'

2   One of you is having a dabbling – with someone else. Forget lipstick on the collar and flowers on the Barclaycard bill. If you want a fail-safe fidelity pointer, check out the Beloved's knicker-drawer. If:

a   there's been a blitz on frayed elastic
b   you discover a concealed lavender sachet
c   there's more than a hint of kink

start worrying.

Am I frivolous, nay absurd, to suggest lingerie reflects libido? Dr John Gayford, Consultant Psychiatrist, who runs a Psycho Sexual Clinic at Warlingham Park Hospital, doesn't think so. According to Dr Gayford it's a 'historical inevitability' that underwear and sex are inextricably entwined. 'Men are prone to fixations,' he explained. 'In the Victorian era when the only bit of female flesh commonly glimpsed was a flash of ankle, they developed fetishes focusing on feet, shoes and boots. These days, if you imagine a young man's sexual exploration, he works from the outside in. He encounters women's underwear long before he makes contact with the female body itself. Many little boys experience their first erections while watching their Mothers dressing. By association, girdles, brassières, even petticoats all become imbued with sexual connotations in their own right.'

Dr Gayford also contends that 'underwear is less threatening than women themselves'. 'Depending on your viewpoint female genitalia can be quite threatening. Some men think of the vagina as a "joybox". (News to me, Ed.)

'To others it's something that often smells, bleeds every month, sometimes emits an unpleasant discharge and, yes, urine passes through it, too. Men who are intimidated by the reality of female sexuality quite often sublimate their feelings into a fascination, or minor obsession with ladies' underwear.'

The ultimate question, of course, is 'Do you keep your underwear on when you do it?' When Al Pacino made Kate Nelligan squeeze her poor feet into bunion-forming gold stilettos throughout intercourse in the film *Frankie and Johnny*, we knew it couldn't possibly be love. When he finally packed the pepperoni with true love Michelle Pfeiffer, he was so starry eyed, he wouldn't have noticed if she'd been wearing DMs. Personally, I'd stick on a snorkel and flippers if I thought it would do any good. Frankly, I'm not averse to squeezing my assets into the occasional black filmy thing in the interest of fanning the conjugal embers, but some women don't take kindly to trussing themselves up like slabs of oven-ready brisket.

As my old school friend elegantly put it: 'Len insists I keep a corset, suspenders, the whole works on while we're making love. At first I didn't mind all that much. It seemed a bit of a lark. But after a few months, I felt completely pissed off and bored brainless with the whole idea. I'd just as soon burn the bloody lot and wear white cotton knickers and a nice sensible bra. Dressing up for sex as if it's a performance is a pain.' On the other hand, my chemist's sister-in-law said: 'If I stuck a pom pom on each nipple and waggled them in front of Nick, he'd tell me I was blocking his view of the telly. I'd love to splash out on saucy bits of lacy stuff, but I'd do better spending my money on a deep fat fryer for all the notice he'd take. He likes easy access, can't be bothered ferreting through all that frou-frou.

Actually, when he's on the job his eyes are tight shut throughout. I'm never sure if he's fantasising about Tina Turner, or if he's fallen asleep. Either way, my undies are lost on him.'

Before you accuse me of sexist stereotyping, I did try. I combed the land, well, Muswell Hill Broadway anyway, searching for a woman who felt strongly about her man keeping his undies on for the duration. I admit it was raining, and I was worried that my hair would frizz up, so I didn't spend hours trawling the streets, but, try as I might, I couldn't find one. Women don't give a damn. Female fetishists are few. We like our lovers *au naturel*, wafting in the breeze if possible. Calvin Klein, BhS or leather jock-strap, it's all the same to us. I suppose, when it all boils down to it, polyester or paisley, balls will be balls.

✿20✿

Does Sleeping In Nowt But A Splash Of Chanel No. 5 Really Do Your Mystique Any Favours?

My Mother's parting words rang in my ears as my husband of six hours and I hailed confetti all over the check-in desk at Gatwick. Before you jump to conclusions, it wasn't a grossly belated birds and bees talk, but something far more lastingly significant. In fact, I'd be reneging on my duty if I failed to repeat it for your edification, so here goes: 'DARLING, AT ALL COSTS, PRE-SERVE YOUR MYSTIQUE.'

Not for my Mother the cosy togetherness of shared toothbrushes and communal combs. Not for my Father mingled toe-nail clippings, mutual bathwater and spaghetti slurped straight from the tin. Not for either of them a duet of flossing, vomiting or burping in tandem. Just to give you an idea, they've been married thirty-five years and she's never once been to the loo with him in the postal district, let alone the house.

Having been foolish enough to marry for love, we lacked the spondulicks for an epic honeymoon. Moroni-cally, we foresook Elysian Bournemouth for a festering Mediterranean dungeon where we fed each other alternate dollops of smoked salmonella. OK, it tasted of garlic armpit, but so did everything else in that oil-soused shit-hole. Innocents abroad, we canoodled on our beach towel, unknowingly finger feeding each other disease on toast. 'A morsel for you, Cherry-Thighs.' Kiss. Kiss. 'A tidbit for you, Thunderballs.' Eight hours later dysentery had turned our bowels to water – green water. My husband was hovering between primitive Mediterranean khazi and rudimentary Mediterranean bidet, puking and crapping simultaneously. What was I doing? Preserving my mystique, of course. Holding back till your husband's vacated the *en suite* can be tough enough on a chilly afternoon in Wolverhampton, in the throes of salmonella it's excruciatingly character building. I rolled round the floor in spasms of gut-wrenching agony, but, hey Mum, it was worth it, he still doesn't realise I do Number 2s.

Naturally, the Mystique Preservation Society is militantly anti-menstrual. The party line is that the merest glimpse of a box of Super Tampax at the back of the bathroom cabinet is enough to extinguish a man's desire forever. Received wisdom has it that although men might, aeons ago, in some dingy school science lab, have heard rumours to the effect that women bleed once a month, they sensibly take the view that this is just too profoundly yukky to be possible. And if, by some vampirish quirk of the Divine imagination, this gruesome phenomenon turns out to be occurring with revolting regularity in a woman of whom they have biblical knowledge, they'd much rather not have the slightest inkling. Thus was born the little plastic box, specifically created to disguise tampons on their trip to the loo. Although I have always wondered what else that shape we're supposed to have fooled men into thinking we're toting to the ladies. The options are strictly limited. We're talking cigars or frankfurters. Call me

Don't forget the socially acceptable menstrual euphemism. 'Suppose a bonk's out of the question?' 'Sorry, not tonight, it's . . .

- my little visitor
- that time of the month
- red flag day
- women's troubles
- the curse

unhinged, but I think I'd prefer to be a known Tampon Carrier, than a closet lavatorial frankfurter chewer.

The period prince

It could be said that Prince Charles has contributed colossally to the cause of menstrual rehabilitation. After all, as Camillagaters know, he did say he wanted to be reincarnated as one of Mrs Parker-Bowles' tampons. Quite frankly, though, I don't think the fellow could tell a menstrual cycle from a motor cycle. It comes with being royal. Ask anyone what the Queen and Picasso have in common and they'll give you one answer – blue periods.

Hairy godmother

Menstruating isn't the only thing we do in secret. Want to know another? How about de-fuzzing?

FACT: Women are supposed to be smooth, fragrant and odourless.

FACT: ALL post-pubescent women – barring Icelandic albinos – have noticeably hairy tufts sprouting from our legs, forearms, under-arms, pubic mounds

FACT: Most of us also have a healthy smattering of hairs decorating our nipples, navels, stomachs, inner thighs and toes. Yes, you have. Don't deny it.

FACT: To be caught nipple-plucking by a male is the ultimate betrayal of feminine mystique, deserving of tar and feathering.

FACT: If tar and feathering guaranteed permanent hair removal we'd be queueing round the block for it.

FACT: These tufts are universally referred to as 'super-fluous hair'. Who says so? Superfluous to what? Why are beards Shakespearean, Christ-like, Talmudic, Dionysian, but never, ever 'superfluous'?

FACT: The smoothness fantasy is big business. Battalions of depilationists are riding the recession with ease just yanking unwanted short and curlies out of female thighs. HANDS UP IF YOU BOOK IN FOR A WEEKLY CHIN TO KNEE WAX. If they're not dropping boiling wax on our bikini line, they're injecting diathermy currents down our fol-licles. Let no-one tell you the route to hairlessness is pain free. Personally, I'd rather have an internal examination than a leg wax, and I know I'm not alone. Hair dissolving cremes are equally unnerving. Stench of charred flesh apart, more bathroom carpets have been dissolved by flying blobs of Immac than I've had cottage cheese and crispbread lunches.

What about the planet?

Every day hundreds of millions of good, strong, super-fluous hairs are simply being thrown away. Discarded. Into the wheelie with 'em. But I would like to raise a question. Is this procedure ecologically sound? Surely, in this era of ecological awareness, something could and should be done on the RECYCLING front. With a little intelligent planning, possibly along the lines of a nationwide competition under the aegis of the Design Council, these resources could be used to benefit society in a myriad of vital ways. A few spring to mind immediately. Biodegrable pre-permed false eyelashes, for example. Or what about wigs with that trendy Naomi Campbell look? Or warm, snug, fun fur

collars to update last year's Winter coat?

A couple we know got divorced and my Mother said: 'Well, I wasn't surprised, she never even wore a nightdress.' It might help to remember that nightdresses were a vital part of my Father's lingerie empire. Right through the heatwave of 1976, my sister, Mother and I steamed uncomplainingly in our swampy polyester satin with rosebud trim. After all, as Dad quite rightly explained, if the entire country flung its brushed nylon to the winds, we'd be out of detached splendour and into the gutter within a week. Nonetheless, my Mother isn't a nightdress enthusiast purely for material reasons. Mystique, as usual, plays a voluminous part. 'Darling, every woman, from a Botticelli goddess to Ursula Andress looks a lot more attractive with a swathe of something diaphanous bunched up round her vitals. At least it leaves a little something to the imagination. We might prefer to be irresistibly appeal-ing in the nude, but, let's take a reality check. Do you look better in:

a   a Chanel suit
b   your birthday suit?

I defy any woman, with the singular exception of Claudia Schiffer, not to choose a. Mystique is all about the suggestion, never the obvious.'

All of which is brill until you reconnoitre the nightwear available in the British Isles. With an exemption for Janet Reger, there's a wretched assembly of turquoise bri-nylon and distended T-shirts with cartoon embellishment. I may be more saggy than shaggy, but I'd pit my cellulite against those passion killers, superfluous stomachs and all.

Common scents

Marilyn Monroe embraced presidents in nothing but a splash of Chanel No. 5. I tend to favour the slightly stale aroma of Tesco cod nuggets and oven chips, mingled with Macleans myself. There's no escaping it. Shower, though we might, you can't be a Mother and not smell of last night's dinner. Spraying with duty frees has no impact on the phenomenon. Seriously, you could pour me a bath of asses' milk and I'd come out ponging of banana Nesquik.

❦ 21 ❦

Stockings And Suspenders
(Or, Deep-Frozen Gussets Meet
Goosepimpled Thighs)

 Which three words are enough to arouse entire generations of British men?

a   love and marriage
b   law and order
c   Value Added Tax
d   Morecambe & Wise
e   stockings and suspenders
f   Marks & Spencer
g   fish and chips
h   Sir Bob Geldof
i   rubber and leather
j   mind the gap
k   cash and carry

No contest. There's a slight frisson for Morecambe & Wise, but the overwhelming vote goes to e. We expect nothing less. We'd consider men irredeemable perverts if they showed an unnatural interest in, say, crimplene blouses, but we confidently assume all normal red blooded males ignite at the merest mention of S and S. To hear some of them tell it, sex without stockings is like an egg without salt. To hear some women tell it, they'd rather lay an egg than a stocking-fancier.

The battle of the sexes never rages more ferociously than over the S and S debacle. Most sane women abhor stockings and suspenders because the suspenders either ride right up your bum crack or go 'ping' at agonisingly inopportune moments, such as:

1   one's own ordination as a Church of England priest
2   one's erudite-yet-touchingly-humble Nobel Prize for Literature acceptance speech
3   one's kissy-kissy procession through Langan's pursued by paparazzi
4   canapés with Andrew Neil

What's more, stockings and suspenders mean:

- one can't climb on a bus without flashing one's mons veneris
- icy blasts whistling round one's thighs
- acute temperature fluctuations inside and outside knickers
- feeling like one of those oven ready roasts with bits of string knotted round them

Most sane men adore stockings and suspenders because:

- Cor!
- Nudge! Nudge!
- Oooh! Aaaah! Cantona!

and other cogent reasons.

Some people don't mind wearing S and S. These include:

a   thrush (vaginal fungus) sufferers – apparently tights

FAMOUS S & S WEARERS

- Lady Bienvenida *uck
- Fiona 'five times a night' Wright
- Julian Clary
- Sam 'I earn more than the Prime Minister' Fox
- Eddie Izzard
- Linda 'I'm a TV presenter now' Lusardi
- Dame Edna Everage
- Pamela 'make mine *The Sunday Times*' Bordes
- Teresa 'ten indecent proposals a day' Gorman MP
- Dustin Hoffman/Robin Williams

FAMOUS NON-S & S WEARERS

- Germaine Greer
- David Bellamy
- Camille Paglia
- Dennis Healey
- Norma Major
- Ryan Giggs
- Our Cilla
- Jeanette Winterson
- Trevor MacDonald

create exactly the warm, moist, cosy environment to make pesky private part yeasts feel thoroughly at home

b   Tory MPs of both sexes

c   bimbos – no such thing as a kiss'n'tell without obligatory S and S pictures to pad out raunchy revelations

d   Readers' Wives – no point his sending in murky Polaroids of your tired old twat without S and S and an erotic backdrop of anaglypta and an appalling repro of 'The Hay Wain'

e   batty old bags who don't realise tights have been invented yet

f   trophy wives – S and S are part of the job description

g   Hollywood actors pretending they're only doing it 'because it's vital for the part'

Let's get to the crotch of the matter. Stockings and suspenders are so sublimely uncomfortable, impractical and disempowering – you try discussing Projected Sales Forecasts with someone who's just heard your suspender 'ping' – women who wear them have to be 'only after one thing'. Stands to reason S & S wearers must be hot stuff. If they were only tepid, lukewarm, room temperature stuff, they'd be in opaque tights and flat pumps like the rest of us. Most men still don't quite believe 'nice girls' are capable of actually enjoying sex. (They have a point. Most men are such lousy lovers, most women would rather have a marshmallow and a Barbara Cartland.) So they're titillated beyond belief by 'bad girls'. But how do you tell a bad girl in a crowd? Fortunately, there are classic bad girl badges, the nympho-equivalent of Hermes' scarves on a Sloane.

Of course, S & S are top of the Bad Girl Tit Parade alongside:

- white stilettos
- gold chains round the ankle
- indelible buttock tattoos
- black roots/peroxide combo
- cheap perfume
- Farrah Fawcett hairdos
- dangly earrings
- inch-thick lip-gloss

The only problem is that most men are seriously terrified of Bad Girls because

a   you might catch something
b   you might be caught catching something
c   they're invariably related to someone with a Dober-
    man called 'Terminator'
d   they've got too much to compare you with
e   they might sell the story to the *Sunday Sport* and make
    you a household name – Limp Larry
f   they might put your back out

Tie and die

What's more, men are scared stiffless a voracious bad girl will tie them to the bed-post with her stockings, escape to Monte Carlo with their credit cards and leave them there stark bollock naked.

So most men settle down with nice girls and waste huge amounts of time and money trying to persuade them to tog up like bad girls. Marks & Spencer, for example, confirm that every Christmas/Valentine's Day thousands of husbands nationwide snap up scarlet basques, suspender belts and bras and next shopping day, thousands of wives nationwide exchange them for a really useful knitted cardigan.

It seems S and S enthusiasts divided neatly into two cups. The A cup are big on luxury. The B cup are heavily into sleaze. A Cups are Janet Regerites, turned on by the decadent thrill of spending enormous sums on scraps of silk only their lovers will ever see. B Cups, using porno mags as their role model, snap up enough schmutters[1] to transform a respectable semi into a little corner of an Amsterdam bordello. A cup membership is fifty–fifty male and female. All the women who say: 'I spend £40 on each pair of La Perla suspenders, but I do it for myself. It's for my own satisfaction, simply a sign of self respect,' are A cups. All the men who stampede through Harvey Nichols in pursuit of £450 negligée sets are A Cups. To them underwear is a logical extension of flowers, Ferraris and Ferragamos, and if you're one of them, feel free to write to me c/o Little, Brown, my publishers.

B cups are 98 per cent male. Sleaze is pretty much strictly for the boys. Whatever their partners pretend to believe, peekaboo bras cut off circulation in the boobs. Thonged G-strings disappear up both gullies, and there's never a convenient time to fish them out again. What's more, pseudo whoreish underwear is ugly as all hell. Shoddily made, prone to virtual instant disintegration, it's not all that cheap and not in the slightest cheerful. Surprisingly, though, some women are sleaze converts.

Suzanne, (of course it's not her real name, I don't want to be sued thank you very much) whose husband can't

[1] 'schmutter' is Yiddish for 'item of clothing your Mother would never have allowed you to buy and you wouldn't have bought either, if you had any sense'.

resist mail ordering everything from wet-look bras to dry-look knickers admitted: 'Frankly, I used to be horrified. It's basically crap. A load of rubbish. Total tat. My daytime look is very Nicole Farhi. Natural fibres. Understated. Elegant, I hope. The underwear Max (not his real name either) wanted me to wear couldn't be more different from my own taste. The colours are vile, the fabrics scratchy and horrible. I resisted for ages. Until one night, after a few Remy Martins, he persuaded me to pose for photographs in one of the outfits. I'd never, in a million years, have predicted this, but when I saw the pictures, I couldn't deny that I found them hot. I looked like a tart. I looked ****ing sexy. Perhaps it was the contrast between this creature and my normal self, who knows? But gradually, I started to realise kinky underwear gives me a sort of freedom. In it, I'm not myself. That frees me to enjoy things I wouldn't normally even try. Max says that's what he had in mind all along.'

If you've got kinky shenanigans in mind, turn, without passing Go or collecting £200 to Chapter 22.

DID YOU KNOW (I CERTAINLY DIDN'T)?

Marks & Spencer buy enough knicker elastic every year to stretch TWICE around the circumference of the world!

✿22✿

Like A Rubber Ball I'll Come Bouncing Back To You

On balance, I'm in favour of sex. It's cheap, low calorie and you don't have to whip up a roulade, Hoover behind the settee or send out invitations. Or do you? Last week along with bills: gas and phone; threats: Bank Manager, an irate reader and a cervix-pink Smear Reminder Form, Postman Pat delivered an invitation to a Rubber Ball. No, it wasn't piggy-in-the-middle day at Toys R Us. I'm talking genuine latex knickers time. Strictly by invitation only. Mystery location to be revealed only on payment of several crisp oncers. (I nearly said 'smackers', but more of that later.) Need I add that I'm not a Rubber Ball mailing list regular? It was strictly work, you understand. I was going to be filming Fetishists At Frolic with a television crew.

Meanwhile, I was cool. It takes more than a waistcoat made of old tyres to ruffle the Feltz feathers. I've read *Men Only*. Hell, I've WRITTEN for *Men Only*! I'm sexually emancipated. I've done IT with the light on. I come from a family of ferocious fornicators. Goddammit, my Father imported the first ever pair of edible panties to Great Britain. (Pineapple flavour, since you ask.) If you'd casually inquired, 'Vanessa, which of the following do you find most offensive (a) a rubber of bridge (b) a rubber band (c) a rubber fetishist?' I'd have plumped straight for (a), no question, I loathe card players. Rubber? Leather? Frankly, they could have been wrapped in aluminium foil with a carrot in every orifice for all I cared. Get my split crotch gusset in a twist? Not I.

All was fine and dandy until I disembarked at some subterranean hideout in the bowels of Brixton, gave the password 'Submission!' and found myself face to buttock with a genuine flesh and blood rubberite. And when I say flesh, believe me, I mean butchers' shops of the stuff. Remember cat's cradle – the finger macramé game we used to play at school with bits of odd string? Well, she was wearing it. Her outfit was nothing but a complicated arrangement of shoelaces. One grazed her nipples. Another slid up between her behind – or behind her between, I'm sure you get the picture. But, baby, I hadn't seen nothin' yet. One chap, completely naked apart from a minute pouch covering what must have been his minute willie and testicles, tapped me on the shoulder, thrust a cat 'o' nine tails into my slippery mitt and whimpered: 'Beat me, please, I deserve it. I've been a very naughty boy.' I mumbled my refusal, but a blonde in stockings, suspenders, boots and rubber corset with bare bosoms jutting over the top, happily obliged. I was still only three feet from the front door.

I'm not sure if it was the whipping post, complete with manacles and chains, in the middle of the room, or the fellow walking around in a leather skirt and a gas mask that did it. But when the producer thrust a rubber dress the size of a tea bag at me and barked: 'Get yourself into this,' my cool started hotting up in a big way. There are times – few, I know – when being a size 16 is a positive blessing. 'Sorry mate, there's no way I'll fit into that thing.' I said, jauntily.

'It's rubber, you moron, it stretches!' And it did. Now I know how it feels inside a condom. I looked a dead ringer for an inflatable black pudding. 'OK, old girl', I told myself, 'now's the time to unleash your sense of humour.' Only I didn't have one. Nothing whatsoever about the Rubber Ball seemed remotely funny. I found it ghastly, embarrassing, humiliating and uncomfortable. I've never been more amazed at myself.

How could I, the unshockable, be shocked to smithereens? Haven't I always defended to the death everyone's right to dress up in net curtains, icing sugar, milk bottles or whatever they fancy and plunge vigorously into sexual activity with the consenting adult of their choice? Of course I have, but, so far, I've defended it purely in THEORY. I haven't exactly been what you'd call a hands-on sexpert. I've been married for nine years and I have to confess, if we summon up the energy to break out of the mish posish once a month, we award ourselves post-coital KitKats for effort. If there is a seamy sexual subculture throbbing in NW10 then it's throbbing bloody quietly. As far as I know bunging on a pair of rubber gloves to save my French manicures from the washing-up is as kinky as it gets round here. In fact, someone mentioned S & M to a friend of mine at a dinner party, and she nudged her husband and said: 'S & M, darling. Haven't we got shares in that?'

I may chuck words like: 'voyeur', 'exhibitionist', 'fetishist' and 'pervert' into the conversation with wanton abandon, but it doesn't mean I have the faintest familiarity with the real thing. Let's face it, to me, decadence is being behind locked bedroom doors, doing exactly what we usually do, with a dollop of raspberry jam on the top. Frankly, flashing my labia in a Brixton basement full of strangers while half strangling myself on a studded leather dog collar has never been high on my list of ambitions.

Yes, you read it correctly. There were exposed labia all over the place. One tattooed 'SLAVE OF MASTER NICK'. Yes, you did have to get pretty close to read it but she didn't seem to mind. Anything and everything hanging out was pierced. I saw pierced nipples, pierced winkles, pierced labia, pierced tongues, pierced lips and pierced eyelids for goodness sake. Here a bottom, there a bosom, everywhere the mingled stench of sweat and rubber. The more I saw, the worse I felt and I was appalled. Me, a prude? Me a narrow minded, prejudiced bigot? Miserably, I phoned my husband. 'I'm at this Rubber Ball and I hate it. Can you come and give me some moral support? Just one minor thing, though. There's a dress code. You'll have to wear your leather jacket and a jock-strap – nothing else – or they won't let you in.'

Did he join me? Like greased sodding lightning. Did he join me in disgust/horror/revulsion? Not a bit of it. ME: 'Isn't this horrific, like your worst nightmare come to life?' HIM: 'Well, I wouldn't say that.' ME: 'Well, what the hell would you say?' HIM: 'You're reacting like an eleven-year-old. Grow up.' In front of us stood a clutch of female gargoyles. Slim, and under twenty-five, their scalps were shaven and tattooed, their eyebrows plucked to oblivion, their lips painted black, mottled areas of their bodies seeped out of rubber hot pants. ME: 'Would you find them more attractive with hair, without tattoos, and in bikinis?' HIM: 'No.' Guess who's going to be draping herself fetchingly in the shower curtain in future?

What kind of person struts their stuff at a Rubber Ball? Architects, bricklayers, teachers, nurses, landscape gardeners and at least one vicar. No one was sure who, but rumour had it the two masked male skirt-wearers were

MPs – and, on present performance, who am I to doubt it? Why would grown up people schlep all the way to Brixton on a Saturday night to thrust their pierced honeymoon tackle at the world? 'Escapism' was the most popular explanation. Sid X explained: 'Here, dressed like this, I can be anyone I want to be.' 'But why do you want to wear a bath mat and wave your willy around at people you don't know?' 'It's the fantasy into reality factor. The universe is divided into exhibitionists and voyeurs, this way we can all indulge without doing any harm to anyone.' Isn't all this S & M paraphenalia, whips, stocks, studs and everything desperately violent and frightening. 'Not at all. S & M is about trust, and understanding, inflicting pain only when mutually agreeable, and only within acceptable limits.'

He had a point. Women bounced unmolested at the Rubber Ball. 'We are completely safe from unwanted approaches in this environment,' explained one thigh-booted, body-stockinged accountant. 'If people don't like it, they don't have to come.' Too true. Gropers are non-existent, gawpers put off by the strict dress code. The rubberites have no wish to inflict their tastes on Joe Public. You won't find them, chains akimbo, in Sainsbury's. Logically, I'm glad they're having fun. Emotionally, I couldn't handle it at all. A week later, I was still having nightmares. I've never been so thoroughly freaked out. Frankly, I could have gone happily to my grave without ever reading a message off another woman's vagina. So, I stand before you, a charlatan, an impostor – a sexpert who prefers her fantasies at home, in private, in Marks & Spencer's pyjamas.

TAKE ME ...
...home!

More
Slimmed
Against
Than
Slimming

23

Love Me, Love My Love Handles

I didn't mean to, but I've become a semi-famous fat person. Whenever they can't get Dawn French, they haul out Feltz. Before you say it, I'll say it. Of course I'd rather be a semi-famous exquisitely beautiful/ravishingly graceful/supremely intellectual person. As my Father says most hours on the hour: 'For this we sent you to Cambridge?' Billowing to a generous 16–18 was hardly a career ploy. I didn't sit there, think 'Right, there's Dawn, Roseanne Arnold, Hattie Jacques – no, she's dead. OK, gap in the market. Target those Mars Bars, girl.' I discovered contentment and crème brûlée and the pounds piled on gradually. Of course, my Mother takes my weight entirely personally. She's convinced I could be a Kate Moss clone if only I wasn't staging a belated teenage rebellion. Every time I eat tiramisu in public she says: 'How can you do this to your Father?' Four years ago, I made my first ever radio broadcast. Greater London Radio. It was witty. It was pithy. The capital was on its knees before me. Elated, I dropped into Mum and Dad's. 'Mum, Dad, how was it?' 'Darling, Sweetheart, your Mother and I are unanimous. Go on the grapefruit diet!' What were they trying to tell me? There wasn't enough room for me in their Hitachi? Were chunks of my thighs splurging from The World At One all the way into The Archers? Or have I got a fat voice? Maybe that's it? Imagine the listeners: 'Switch off, Harold. She's a size 18 if ever I heard one.' Basically, when you're too fat for RADIO you've hit rock bottom.

I'll tell you when I first realised I had what's commonly known as 'a weight problem', suddenly I couldn't drink a Fat Coke in public. It's a fact of life that fat people are forced to flaunt their Diet Cokes. A can of Diet Coke says: 'OK, I know I'm fat and I'm sorry.' Have you noticed a fat person never eats cheesecake without ordering a can of Diet Coke first? Why? Because the Diet Coke's shorthand for: 'All right, I'm not Cindy Crawford, but think how much fatter I'd be if I'd ordered a Fat Coke with this.' The other night, I snuggled up to my husband and purred: 'Darling, you can tell me honestly, do you think I'm overweight?' His reply? 'Of course not, Cherub. Now get back to your own three quarters of the bed and let me get some sleep.'

Don't think I haven't tried dieting. It's like glue sniffing and beating up old ladies, one of those juvenile delinquencies we all go through. About ten years ago, I went on this special fourteen day diet – and all I lost was two weeks. Then I tried the Banana Diet, and put on half a stone. Don't be fooled by appearances. A banana is a cream cake masquerading as a fruit. To tell you the truth, my house is bursting with diet books: *Hip and Thigh, Bum and Tit, F and Blind, Start and Fart*. Actually, you could poach them all lightly in a little lemon juice and you'd end up with the definitive diet: If It Tastes Halfway Decent, Spit It Out! As far as I'm concerned, life's too short to eat salad. What's more, big women are far more capable of loving, lusting and being downright bedroomly disgusting. After all, we've polished off a proper breakfast. Cottage cheese is fine for foreplay, but serious sex takes stamina.

Is it possible for a woman to be fat and sexy? Of course it bloody is. Use your eyes, for God's sake. Forty-seven per cent of British womanhood is size 16 plus. We forty-seven per centers know full well we're being blissfully wedded, passionately bedded and permanently panted over. We're no celibates, soulfully sucking celery sticks in solitary confinement. Remember, real men don't read *Vogue*. They don't realise they're supposed to fancy skeletal skinnies who'd look most comfortable on Third World Aid posters. Bones are beautiful? Sure they are. To orthopaedic surgeons and gay fashion designers whose ideal woman most closely resembles a clothes hanger.

It's true that I could shed a few stone. My husband says my bosoms look like a bottom. If my bosoms look like a bottom, what does my bottom look like? Don't answer that. I found out. And I curse the hotel chain that installs wall sized mirrors at lavatory level. Bastards! Aren't women oozing enough self-hatred without being forced to confront our buttocks every time we pay a call of nature? So I'm hardly a hot contender for fairest one of all. Unless, that is, you happen to be Rubens. I'm definitely drop dead gorgeous above the lips and below the knees, though. What's more, you could do far worse than write home about my shapely elbows and elegant wrists. The rest, Gentle Reader, is billowing mush. Stretchmarked flaps of belly roll down over my briefs and when I forget to tilt my chin alluringly à la Dietrich a second spreads out under the first like a Hovercraft cushion. Listen, my cellulite's got cellulite. I wouldn't be caught full frontal in a communal changing room for all the bargains at Brent Cross.

That said, can I possibly think I'm sexy? Think so? No. I know I am and so do you. The twelve thousand 'This Morning' viewers who called in can't all be myopic maniacs (I hope). I wrote an article called 'I'm Big and I'm Sexy' for *SHE* Magazine. Weeks later, in front of 3.5 million viewers, I was forced to face the music. 'Is Vanessa sexy?' Richard and Judy asked the nation. I sat in the corner with a paper bag over my head, shaking, wishing I was Joan Bakewell, bracing myself for an avalanche of 'Get that fat slag of the screen!' calls. They never came. Instead, I basked in approval, admiration and refreshingly lurid indecent proposals. Six months later, the same thing happened again in New York. The Maury Povich Show asked me to take part in a programme called 'The Fat Myth'. Would I be flown out, stretch limousined and Fifth Avenue hotelled? Would I? I bought a few cans of beans and an opener, showed the kids how to work it and caught the first Virgin outta here. Thirty-two thousand feet up, I asked myself the 64 million dollar question. Why did they need to schlep Fattie Feltz all the way over the pond from NW10? We've seen Mr and Mrs Michelin-Middle-America taking their Dunkin' Donuts intravenously. Why didn't they just dig up a home-grown Stateside podge to jiggle her thingies for Maury?

American TV is a hot and cold running freak show. Coming up after these messages: 'The Man Who Committed Acts Of Indecency With A Thanksgiving Turkey' and 'I'm In Love With My Own Grandpa!' Of course, there's one thing all those perverts, psychos and sickos have in common. They're all size 14 or under. Fattism is so rife, body fascism so ingrained, it's positively un-American to be fat and happy. Cue Feltz.

If you can't imagine any male in his right mind fancying fat, blame Hollywood. Celluloid sex doesn't happen to anyone over a size 10. The man who pays the Pfeiffer calls the tune. Julia Roberts' grizzini-thin grapplings have rammed it into our suggestible minds that multi-orgasmic equals virtually anorexic. We're talking seriously lethal hip bones, ribs like pre-gnawed rack of lamb and curiously inverted thighs that curve inwards. In films, fat people are inevitably cast as pals – take a bow ubiquitous fat friend – never lovers. If the earth moves for a fattie, she's never pounding away on top of Michael Douglas. Ten to one you're watching *Earthquake*.

In life, Thank God, sex is like chocolate mousse. A rammekin-full is nice. A massive vat of the stuff is even nicer. Men who genuinely love women fantasise about being smothered in sofa sized breasts and pillowed in marshmallow thighs. Pert is OK, pneumatic is Heaven. Not for them the bite sized chunk. They revel in handfuls and fistfuls and armfuls of lusty lady. Of course, billions of chaps don't actually like women very much. They'll only tolerate us emaciated, depilated and deodorised. Pregnancy turns them off. They'll only contemplate grudging cunnilingus with a clothes peg clamped over their noses. Men who count your calories, slap your hand as it inches towards the Maltesers and stand over you with a stop watch while you do your sit-ups, invariably claim to be doing it for your own good. Tosh! They're woman haters. Flesh fearing, fat baiting misogynists. They don't fancy me. Rest assured, the repugnance is entirely mutual.

⟨24⟩

Every Woman Knows Tiramisu Is Better Than Sex, So Why Not Combine The Two?

It was Mother Theresa, Mrs Patrick Campbell, Jerry Hall or someone along those lines who said: 'A woman should be a chef in the kitchen, a lady in the drawing room and a whore in the bedroom.' I'm not altogether sure about this. I mean, wouldn't you rather provide conjugals free, and charge for cooking? What's a hand job between friends? You can at least watch Inspector Morse while you're jerking his gherkin. But a cheese soufflé? We're talking substantial sacrifice. Cooking is not my field. It is strictly as a consumer that I excel.

I love food. Often more than sex. Sex is so unreliable. A plate of thinly sliced pastrami never lets you down. I could claim my ultimate sensual smorgasbord is a combination of the two, but frankly, that's a red herring (delicious with raw onion on pumpernickel). The truth is, presented with an à la carte fantasy – sucking goulash off Sylvester Stallone's triceps – I'd probably go straight for the stew and put Rambo on hold. New York comedian Jackie Mason is famous for his poignant lament: 'We had sex, but we didn't have soup yet.' He has a point. A good feel will never replace a good meal. Face it, woman cannot live by bed alone. Carnal appetites definitely stem from calorific stoking. I'm talking serious sin food, you understand. Crispbread and Slimasoup have a zero Big O factor. I've never seen a survey on the subject, but I'm willing to bet my Welsh rarebit recipe more orgasms are achieved after shepherd's pie and sticky toffee pudding than on an empty stomach.

Am I a food fan? Absolutely. So, am I a Foodie? Give over. I don't care if my olive oil's extra virgin, or downright promiscuous. Raspberries, in my vocabulary, come pulverised in jars of Hartley's, not bobbing about inside £8 bottles of balsamic vinegar. Wild salmon? Listen, I don't mind if it's delinquent as long as there's plenty of Hollandaise. Suburban dinner parties these days are the gastronomic equivalent of Mastermind. As the hostess struggles in under piles of genuine Provençal earthenware, captive eaters break into a cold sweat. Eight Harvey Nichols, Italianate baroque gold-plated spoons are immersed in a brackish liquid the colour and consistency of untreated sewage. Nervous tongues dart out, ferreting hopelessly in the anxious quest for clues. The foolhardy property developer on your right plunges in: 'Selina, do I detect a touch of arugula?' he asks with the poignant bravado of a man doomed to failure. Relishing every piquant instant, Selina pours herself a spot of blood temperature Badoit – practically indistinguishable from dirty washing up water with a witty trickle of worn-out Fairy Liquid, if you ask me – and laughs derisively. Impetuously, the recession-shattered broker on your left erupts: 'Courgette and brie, with boursin instead of the brie and American squash, thickened with Jerusalem artichoke to mellow the courgettes,' he declares with kamikaze resignation. Selina sniggers: 'Close Roger, but not close enough.'

double dipping into
mint sauce
grasping bone in
fingers
allowing fat to run
down chin
smacked lips
second helpings
dessert
siesta

Your host, a soupçon the worse for being forced to act as official taster during the intensive run up to the banquet, slips in a handful of Rennies under cover of milling a few rounds of freshly harvested pepper noire. Rather lamely, I chip (or should I say *pomme frite*) in with a feeble: 'I'm sure there's a trace of cayenne in here somewhere.' No comment. Either you're right, or she'd rather die than admit she used common or *jardin* Waitrose. After a wretched interval during which guests attempt to swallow the glutinous pottage by bolting down chunks of ciabatta so hard it must have been hewn from genuine carrara marble, Camilla opposite speaks out. With the authoritative air common to Prue Leith academy graduates, Camilla reveals: 'Peruvian version of vichyssoise. Quite simple. Plenty of shallots with the oregano. *Crème fraîche*, not Greek yoghurt. I would have introduced a stonger undercurrent of parsnip to counteract the sweetness of the leeks? What do you think, Charlotte?'

Charlotte contends that a sprig or two of dried bulgar-wheat adds to the audacity of the *mélange*. Douglas is torn between the unadulterated brutality of pureed turnip and the seduction of the taste-buds afforded by a smattering of sunflower seeds. Impassioned debate ignites the table. While turmoil rages, the entrée is served. A single furled mange tout frames three transparent slivers of sole, treading water in a verdant puddle of aubergine coulis. Acres of empty plate gleam up at you. If no-one was watching, you'd spear the whole sodding lot and down it in one. As it is, you prolong the process by dissecting the duck, filleting the mange tout and trawling the coulis. Delaying tactics notwithstanding, two minutes later you've polished off the lot. Garnish? You've eaten it. What about the little bundle of string on everyone's side plates. The one used to bind up the duck breast? Bugger it. Eaten that too. Best bit of the meal, really. At least it wasn't stuffed with pine kernels.

I don't trust Foodies. I'm not certain they genuinely like eating. I think they're closet guilt trippers, struggling for chocolate covered raisin *d'être* by blinding each other with domestic science. In my experience, people who drone on about vibrators, manacles and French ticklers spend all their time leafing through catalogues and colour co-ordinating their cat-o'-nine-tails. They never get round to having sex at all. The same is true of fully marinaded Foodies. They're forever flashing their spatulas, arguing about Agas, char grilling their polenta and drooling over copper bottomed skillets. They commit chunks of Elizabeth David and Arabella Boxer to memory. They dream about swapping offal stories with Lloyd Grossman. But do they eat? Look at it this way. If making a cheese sandwich means foil wrapping Irish larva bread, oven baking it, lacing each slice with drizzled trails of aioli, dashing to an over-priced/spiced deli for freshly goat-given chèvres, sprinkling on radiccio and worrying like hell about which wine brings out the true rancid nastiness of the ensemble, wouldn't you rather forget the whole thing and curl up with *The Good Food Guide.*

Give me *cuisine grandmère.* The concentrated cholesterol my Grandma Babs used to serve up in Stanmore. Over populated chicken soup with jostling vermicelli, dumplings, floating carrots and kosher wonton. Turkey escalopes as big as your head. Mashed potato so seduced by milk and butter it compensates the eater for not being breast-fed. Pastry that fights each bite, sheltering slightly submissive Coxes, drowning in cinammon. Naturally, every course was served with bread. 'Vanessa, take some

TACKLING
A LAMB CHOP
– BAD SIGNS

surgical amputation of
  all fat
sawing flesh off bone
  with knife
swabbing face with
  Eau de Cologne
  sachet
indigestion
step class
weight training
cold shower

149

bread with that.' 'Grandma, bread? With strawberry ice-cream?' 'Just a little to help wash it down.'

Freud said that all well-adjusted people are partial to food and fornication. Sigmund knew his onions (glazed, with a little brown sugar). Watch a man/woman tackle a lamb chop. They'll tackle you the same way.

Jewish Mothers always tell their children: 'Boobela[1], you're so gorgeous, I could eat you!' That's the perfect training for living happily (not skinnily, but which would you rather be?) ever after. Food is synonymous with love. The more expansive the dish, the more profound the feeling expressed. Call it conditioning, if you will, but to me there is more passion in a steaming vat of cholesterol-packed cholent than in a salad guaranteed to unblock your arteries. Calories are comforting. Five courses are more friendly than four. Food isn't a vice, it's a pleasure. After all, if God had meant us to be skinny, he'd never have invented M & S crème brûlée.

If you fancy making some Boobelas for someone you love, here is Greta Goldwater's recipe: 2 eggs, pinch salt, warm water to mix, 4 tablespoons of fine matza meal, oil – apple slices, cinammon and ground almonds optional.

Beat eggs, salt and 2 tablespoons of water together. Gradually beat in matza meal adding more water to make a thick batter. Heat oil. When oil is really hot, drop in spoonfuls of mixture and turn till brown. Sprinkle sugar on the top. Apple slices, cinammon and ground almonds can be added to the mixture if desired.

---

[1] Boobela is Yiddish for 'Little Darling' and also the name for delicious matza meal dumplings fried in oil.

⊛25⊛

What If You Found Yourself...
And Wished You Hadn't?

I was going to say you wouldn't believe the number of people (many of them close relatives) who've suggested I have therapy to discover and unleash the svelte Feltz trapped inside my fat, but on second thoughts you probably would.

It didn't snuff it in the seventies. The urge festers on. Millions part with upwards of £40 quid an hour for the privilege. Mothers forsake nurseries teeming with flesh of their flesh to do it. Executives flick through their personal organisers wondering which page holds the key. Urbanites are convinced it lies in a hayrick. Rustics stalk it in litter-lined gutters. I'm talking, of course, about the time-honoured pursuit of FINDING YOURSELF.

It's tough being part of the ME generation when you're not sure who you are. Leaving your well-paid job increasing the market share of winged sanitary towels to run a free-range trout farm complete with hand-propelled water mill doesn't always do the trick. One morning, you toss a handful of home-grown basil into your organic muesli and think: 'This is not where I am coming from.' That is your cue to embark on an infinite and exceedingly expensive course of therapy designed to 'put you in touch with yourself'. I mean, why not? You can see what twenty-five

PLACES YOU'RE UNLIKELY TO BUMP INTO YOURSELF

- Club 18-30 (particularly if you're on the autumnal side of spring chicken)
- in the studio audience of 'Don't Forget Your Toothbrush'
- tossing the caber
- tossing anything more interesting
- brass-rubbing classes
- fell walking
- fenn walking
- fjord walking
- walking (As my Mother says: 'Vanessa CAN walk, but thank God she doesn't have to!)
- the Oscars

151

ALL THE BEST
THERAPISTS
HAVE ...

- therapists
- mittel European accents
- overbearing Mothers
- henpecked Fathers
- personalised number plates: ID 17R, EGO 100K
- Hampstead addresses
- traumatised receptionists
- nervous tics
- recessed lighting
- unlimited Kleenex
- womb rooms for rebirthing
- sandpits for regressing
- *Tatler, Harpers* and *Vogue* in the waiting room

years of the stuff did for Woody Allen.

People get almost as snotty about their therapists as they do about their private gynaecologists. In fact, therapy has biffed converted goat pens in Britanny, liveried Norland nannies and two hundred quid Montblanc biros right off the Top Ten Status Symbol Charts. There's something intoxicating about paying someone else to probe your psyche and if (s)he is a Jungian with Freudian tendencies and a Le Corbusier sofa, so much the better. The downmarket alternative to therapy happens at weekends in deserted sixties pre-fab polys. These consist of sitting on the floor with twenty-six fellow searchers and a counsellor and not being allowed out for a pee, lest you break the circle of concentration. Perhaps the pressure of a bursting bladder puts the ego in touch with the id? Fans nominate stumbling blindfold round the room, fondling anyone you happen to collide with in any intimate place you're lucky enough to encounter as a favourite feature.

What astounds me is the optimistic confidence with which people embark on this particular quest. Take it from me, if you were such a big deal you'd have had the gumption to introduce yourself to yourself by now. Why do you think you've been keeping yourself under your hat all these years? Because you're no great shakes, that's why. Contemplate your navel if you must, but don't confuse it with the Nile delta. Why assume that the quintessence of you-ness will turn out to be a delectable composite of Joan of Arc, George Eliot and Julia Roberts? When the breakthrough finally comes and you meet yourself head on, you're far more likely to be the sort of total embarrassment you'd die rather than appear with in public.

It's closely akin to the Hospital Switch Syndrome. Didn't you stagger home from kindergarten, cast a scornful glance at the bourgeoisie doling out the fish fingers and the gormless old duffer yelling: 'Open the box!' at Michael Miles, and console yourself with the certainty that they couldn't possibly be your real Mum and Dad? It was a balls-up by the nurses. If they hadn't been understaffed that day, you'd be bagging a few pheasant on the old estate with Harris the gammy legged game-keeper, or peeling the odd grape at a Hampstead soirée as Mater spouted hexameters and Pater turned out a spot of surrealist sculpture.

Being oneself is hideously painful to accept. Like knowing you'll never be the most beautiful woman in the room. Or coming to terms with a pear-shaped bum. The belief that a swan lurks deep within every duckling was shoved down our unsuspecting gullets along with Marmite fingers. We all know what's supposed to happen when you kiss a frog. When kissing doesn't work we try a bit of the other. When, in the flattering light of the afterglow, he still looks repellantly amphibian, we blame ourselves.

Blame is a vital ingredient in the Finding Yourself menu. The basic premise is that you could have been yourself if only THEY hadn't stopped you. THEY can be anyone from the aforementioned Ma and Pa to the examiners who failed to appreciate the quirky individualism of your Physics O level, to the bastard who allowed you to marry him without completing your diploma in aerobics teaching.

Statistically speaking, finding yourself is a mug's game. Think about it. There is only one ran for every million also-rans. Which are you likely to be? There is only one Superman, but Clark Kents are forming an orderly queue in front of every photocopier in the realm. Checking in to your local Ashram for a weekend break won't turn you into a Someone. Nor will walking barefoot through Regent's Park communing with the lupins. Face it. You're not a

TOP 10
CANDIDATES FOR
TERMINAL BLAME

- Mum
- Dad
- Mum's Mum
- Dad's Dad
- older siblings – for being older
- younger siblings – for being younger
- non-existent siblings – for rivalry-deprivation
- piano teacher - for failing to detect concert potential
- piano teacher – for detecting concert potential and forcing you to practice
- all members of your own sex – for sniggering at you in the changing rooms
- members of the opposite sex – for sniggering at you outside the changing rooms

strangulated media meteor asphyxiating from lack of recognition. Chances are you're as mediocre as the next man.

Anyway, if you really are Nelsons (Mandela and Horatio), Wellingtons (Duke of and boots) and Tynans (Kenneth and Wear) all rolled into one magnificent megalith, what on earth makes you think therapy will coax the hero out of the wimp? You may not have realised this, but therapists don't actually say anything. At all. Ever. That's their job. They sit comfortably in their own homes for fifty minutes – no commute, no pricey office separates to dry clean, no depreciation on the car, no canteen lunch – they utter not a word, and they pocket £40 a throw. No wonder they're so sodding well-adjusted. We'd be feeling pretty darned mellow ourselves if we earned a good living tucked up cosily in the front room saying F. bloody all.

Your therapist is most likely to say . . .

- You think you think that?
- You feel you feel that?
- I'm feeling that you're feeling a lot you haven't felt before?
- I'm thinking that perhaps you're thinking, not feeling?
- I feel for your feelings.
- I hear where you're coming from.
- What are your thoughts on those feelings?
- How do those feelings make you feel?
- You want to sleep with your Father and crucify your Mother? Time's up. That'll be forty pounds, please.

Your therapist is least likely to say . . .

- You are a mad, insane bastard, aren't you!
- I feel exactly the same about my Mother.
- Do you think this shirt brings out the hint of aquamarine in the curtains?
- Who needs therapy when you've got chocolate?
- What's past is past. No point digging up all that old shit now.
- I have this inexplicable fear of light fittings.
- Sure, time's up, but what do I care. Have another half hour on me.

I'd rather go under the knife than have some old ham in a smoking jacket rifling through my emotional baggage. It may have turned me into an Evans Outsize, but at least it's mine. So, life isn't like The Partridge Family. Who said it would be. I'm with Sophocles who pertinently remarked: 'Call no man happy until his death.'

❦26❦

Too Tired For The Twiddly Bits - Leave The Foreplay Till Afterwards, If We've Still Got The Energy

Foreplay is a drag. One of life's dreariest 'Have to's'. On a par with teeth cleaning, learning your French verbs and lagging the loft in the 'If You Don't, You'll Be Sorry' stakes. Life is supposed to be a series of equations. To wax algebraic, BAD + BAD + BAD = GOOD.

For example:

No Sex + No Drugs + No Rock'n'Roll = A Job Presenting GMTV

No Food + No Alcohol + Permanent Halitosis = Size 8 figure

Come From A Broken Home + Speak In A Stupid Voice + Hang Out In Polo Fields = Marry Into The Royal Family

No Bubble Bath + No Holiday + C&A Clothes = Keep Head Above Water

In a society in thrall to the Puritan work ethic, we can't bear anything to 'come easy', and that includes people. When Brits read celeb interviews, we don't waste time dwelling on the his'n'hers heli-pads or the Rolex egg timer. Seduced by the trappings of success? No, sir! We see private islands in the Maldives for the hollow sham they really are. We adore a nice, leisurely linger on the 'Coming Up The Hard Way' section. The harder the better. If the star was one of eighteen orphaned children, lived under a stone and sold his earlobes to pay for acting lessons, we lap it up. If he spent his teenage years in intensive care and his twenties in a salt-mine, before overcoming a crippling speech-impediment, so much the better. No pain, no gain. Sacrifice breeds success. Ninety-nine per cent perspiration, only one per cent inspiration.

'There! What did I tell you?' we nod sagely at each other. 'As ye sow, so shall ye reap.' Of course, most of us are so busy sowing, we haven't got the strength to reap more than a tin of Jolly Green Giant sweetcorn – and that's just the way we like it. After all, if you start all that reaping business, you might well find you could have misspent your youth, squandered your middle years on cocaine and crosswords and your dotage on bad boys with throbbing Harley Davidsons for all the pleasure it gives you.

If there's anything Brits hate worse than foreigners, it's people who make it without suffering. Take a bow ex-Wordie Amanda de Cadenet, who didn't even have the grace to be POOR. You can't be an icon without stigmata. It's no coincidence that Julie Walters used to be a nurse. So did Claire Rayner and Jo Brand. Rod Stewart was a grave-digger, for god's sake. Mandy Smith may not be a Joan Bakewell, but we'll forgive her her TV contract because she suffered Bill Wyman. Cilla may have queened it in stockbroker Surrey for centuries, but we'll never forget that roach-infested Liverpudlian tenement. Princess Di was a virgin when she married the Monstrous Carbuncle and only a reluctant Squidgy, so we'll grant her all the Mercedes and £600 ski-suits her sweet soul desires. Fergie, on the other hand, was putting it about a lot pre-nuptially and having far too fab a time Texan toe-sucking ever to be forgiven. She didn't deserve to be a Princess in a golden Range Rover because she had too much of a blast poking bureaucratic bottoms at Ascot, smooching with Billy Connolly and commissioning crested toasters. We can't stand our figureheads happy. Let the Antipodean sun flame grill 'em while an amphetamined Maori sticks his tongue in their nostrils. Let them watch wall-to-wall Morris dancing and snip the ribbon at prosthetics factories in Sunderland. We love it when the Queen turns up in an eighteen-year-old hat and schleps round turning off the lights at B. Palace. We're ecstatic when Prince Charles collects old soap fragments and mashes them together in a special economical soap-masher. We love it because it confirms the most comforting adage in the world: 'It's impossible to be rich AND happy.'

As in: 'She may have a Fabergé tampon holder, chateau in Biarritz, Vidal flown in specially from LA to tease her Joanna Lumley, and breakfast at Tiffany's – but is she HAPPY?' Before you sink into the realms of cosy cliché, consider my late and very much lamented Grandma Sybil. 'Money never brought anyone happiness,' clucked her friends at the Bridge Club through mouthfuls of smoked salmon bagel. Alone among the matriarchs, Grandma didn't buy it. 'What about Florrie Goldberg?' she rejoindered smartly. Frankly, there wasn't much they could say to that. Florrie Goldberg was, and, God willing, at the time of going to press still is, living proof that it's brill being a Have. Florrie was a rich little rich girl. Now she's an even richer little old lady. The heel never fell out of Goldberg

Socks plc. Florrie didn't end up a sad, lonely millionairess, secretly spiking her chicken soup with vermouth, or braining her husband Izzy with a gefilte fish ball.

All of which brings me most reluctantly back to foreplay. Also known far more accurately as boreplay. Boreplay is society's attempt to ruin sex. Boreplay turns sex into the genital equivalent of 'not having a single bite of sherry trifle until you've eaten all your greens'. Boreplay is the BAD + BAD + BAD we're supposed to offer up to the gods in order to guarantee some GOOD. Boreplay is the Offical Orgasmic Insurance Policy. If you don't lavish sufficient time and imagination on your Boreplay repertoire, you'll only have yourself to thank when you come:

a   too quickly
b   too slowly
c   not at all

There isn't a sexpert on the globe who isn't a vigorous foreplay devotee. Foreplay, they assure us, is the investment we have to make for the pleasure dividend. Failure to commit foreplay is punishable by:

1   mutual frustration
2   communication breakdown
3   marital disintegration
4   annihilation of society as we know it

Conscientious and unflinching foreplay is rewarded by:

1   simultaneous orgasm
2   mutual gratitude
3   household harmony
4   Back To Basics

Q: *Is there an acceptable minimum foreplay time?*

A: Absolutely. Carry on for as long as you're enjoying it. Then add twenty minutes.

Q: *Is there an acceptable foreplay content?*

A: Certainly. Foreplay doesn't qualify as such without laborious shoulder kneading, time-consuming cavity-probing tongue twisters and pouring Johnson's Baby Oil into each others' navels.

Q: *What if I don't feel like it?*

A: Irrelevant. Foreplay exists for your own good. No-one has ever said you're supposed to enjoy it.

Q: *What if there's a Clint Eastwood film on in three minutes?*

A: What do you think videos are for? N.B. If you can't programme yours, ask a neighbouring toddler.

Foreplay, claim the sexperts, is tantamount to:

1 putting anti-freeze in the car
2 cutting off your split ends
3 watching your cholesterol
4 taking library books back on time
5 washing your whites separately

If you don't you've only yourself to blame! So in the 1990s foreplay has become a moral obligation. Non-foreplayers attract all sorts of unflattering adjectives: selfish, inconsiderate, wham-bam-thank-you-Ma'am, only after one thing, to name but a smattering.

OK, we all know foreplay's compulsory. There's just one teensy, weensy little thing we're not quite certain of. Just a minor matter. Nothing to be concerned about. What, exactly, when it's at home, on the bottom line, IS foreplay? Well, I've asked around, and it turns out that one man's foreplay is another man's slap and tickle. In other words, foreplay can be a tweak of each nipple and a brisk pat on the bollocks, or a total body workover commencing with scalp massage, concluding with a grand ankle licking finale. Pundits define foreplay scientifically as 'all the stuff that's supposed to get you in the mood for the other stuff'. Controversy reigns, however.

Perhaps you've gathered I think foreplay is the pits. It was invented by a conspiracy of sexperts to clog us up with yet more guilt and obligation. 'Sex', they say, 'is something you have to work at.' 'Crap!' say I. Work is what you work at. Weedless rose-beds is what you work at. Perfect shortcrust is what you work at. Sex is arguably the ONLY rewarding aspect of life where NO WORK IS NECESSARY. You do (or don't do) it because you do (or don't) want to. You paint butterflies on each other's bums in cochineal because you feel like it, NOT because some old harpie says it's good for you. Comedian Jenny Eclair wrote: 'I'm not that interested in foreplay. If I want a shag, I want a shag. Listen, I'm tired. I have to get up early. I want to come yesterday, thank you.' I wish I'd written that.

🍓27🍓

Putting Your Foot In It

 I don't know about you, but I still haven't quite recovered from the revelation that the toe is the clitoris of the 90s. Without wishing to put too fine a point upon it, I'd always kept mine clamped firmly in my Russell and Bromley's. Apparently, toe jobs are the only kind of oral sex it's possible to indulge in with your knickers on. And, when you think about it, toe jobs are an excellent form of safe sex. Unless, of course, you're worried about catching athlete's lip. Frankly, all this talk of high-profile toe jobs left me questioning my sexual competence. I'd always considered myself sexually emancipated, but the spectacle of the Duchess of York avidly imbibing a Texan toe put me off my stroke for weeks. As if that weren't enough, we were force fed indigestible details of ex-Fun Minister Mellor's penchant for nibbling on Antonia de Sancha's Italianate feet.

Just as the Fergie/Mellor foot fetish was gradually permeating a perplexed British public, professional toe-teaser, Madonna salvaged a bog-boring much-hyped exclusive interview by wickedly inviting Jonathan Ross to a reciprocal digit-chewing session. That did it. Suddenly, I felt hopelessly outside the sexual swim. For all I knew, the entire world had ten mini-orgasmatrons in its socks. Was I the only prude who'd been brought up to avoid putting my foot in it?

Then another worry struck me. Had we only been exposed to the acceptable public face of toe jobs? Was sucking just the tip of the toe-nail? Did toe afficionadoes privately indulge in bizarre, but exquisitely pleasurable, practices? Did they, for example, routinely immerse their toes in a variety of adventurous orifices? Had toes perhaps replaced fingers as the mutual masturbation tool of choice? In short, did the term 'footloose and fancy free' evoke an entire foot-based repertoire of sexual athletics I hadn't even realised I was missing out on?

Never one to shirk a challenge, I dived beneath the duvet and lunged at my husband's you know whats. At this point, I have to confess, I didn't marry him for his feet. Some men, I imagine, have the sort of delectable toes red blooded women yearn to sink their teeth into. Not he. Think chiropodist's nightmare. Think prehensile claws. Think barnacled nails. Think bristling tufts of black hair. Hardly a natural choice of lolipop. Nonetheless, I opened wide and sucked like fury.

Was it fab? At first, he didn't think so. Experienced toe fanciers will know you have to break through the ticklish barrier before serious arousal sets in. Basically, it's an exercise in endurance. If you can manage not to giggle, squeal and yank your foot away, there's a strong chance that distinct frissons of unadulterated bliss will seep through. He was having such a satisfactory time I thought I'd stumbled upon his T-spot! Foot and mouth disease is highly contagious. It wasn't long before I thrust my – somewhat podgy red nail-polished – big toe. Verdict? Delightful.

To boldly go where no tongue has gone before

All of which prompted me to probe the subject's wider implications. Just when you thought it was safe to take your tights off, the toe emerges as every Brit's favourite elevenses. But why stop at feet? What about the unknown zones? Are Britain's more inventive lovers discovering hitherto unprecedented rapture up their nostrils? Are elbows erogenous? Intrigued, I did what any self-respecting journalist would do – asked my friends. (I agree, it is amazing I've still got any!)

BALD SPOTS

Lysette, turned out to be an unknown zone enthusiast. 'We've been toe-jobbing for years. In fact, I can't think of a single inch of Charlie I haven't licked. It's an extension of kissing, really. Actually, the erotic discoveries we've made together over the years have been fascinating. For example, did you know that bald spots and receding hair lines are incredibly sensitive?' Well, no. I hadn't thought about it to be honest. 'Oh, you should. Kiss a man on his bald spot and he shivers. Lick or suck him there and he'll go wild.'

SHE Magazine published my Guide to Toe Jobs and the Unknown Zones and the tabloids went demented. The *Sun*'s headline read: 'DON'T BE A THICKIE, GIVE A BALDIE A LICKIE!' Possibly the finest moment of my career to date.

ORGASMIC EARLOBES

Nikki was equally positive. 'You mean you don't know about earlobes?' she asked, aghast. 'Even Desmond Morris in *The Naked Ape* goes on about the only purpose of lobes being sexual. They don't serve any other biological function. They're loaded with nerve endings and it's quite common for people to achieve orgasm simply through having their earlobes gently bitten or sucked.' Has she ever climaxed that way? 'Not exactly. But there does seem to be a definite link-up between the lobes and the vagina. When Dan nibbles my lobes everything else starts moistening like mad. Of course, men are equally susceptible. Flicking Dan's ear (not just the lobe, inside too) with the tip of my tongue virtually guarantees an erection.'

EROTIC ELBOWS

Any advance on toes, bald spots and earlobes? Not so much an advance as a veritable deluge. Twice married Suzanne remembered a holiday interlude with a YSL-suited Parisian. 'We were sitting in a brasserie on the Rive Gauche. He took my hand. I was sure he was going to do the cliched thing and kiss the back of it like a crummy pastiche of Maurice Chevalier. 'This is going to be naff,' I thought, and steeled myself to loathe it. But he didn't do anything of the kind. Instead, he luxuriously traced a path with his tongue all the way from the tip of my middle finger to the crook of my elbow. That crease on the inside of the elbow is a wow! I jumped right out of my chair. He taught me that practically every part of the body is capable of a sexy response. My only problem since then has been trying to get British men to experience life outside the missionary position.'

NAVEL NIRVANA

Dave, 43, married with three kids is a confirmed navel licker. 'People tend to think navel = dried up umbilical cord = yeuch. It's a shame because I've yet to meet a woman who didn't absolutely adore having her belly button French kissed. All right. I know it sounds stupid. But it's more convenient than toe sucking, and twice as much fun.' Men, it seems, find tummy button twiddling irresistible. 'To be honest, the navel IS an orifice. Granted, it's a short one. But as far as I'm concerned all our orifices are designed to give sexual pleasure and the navel is no exception.' (N.B. I tried this one. Dave definitely has a point.)

KNOCK KNEES

Surely I'd exhausted the issue? No-one was going to rush in with a last minute nomination for the eyebrow? Or were they ..? Karen confessed to: 'Literally going weak at the knees.' Apparently, 'going down on bended knee' doesn't necessarily mean what you'd expect it to. Karen wasn't the only one to wax lyrical about responsive qualities of knee-backs. Amy agreed. 'Would you believe, my knees are more sensitive than my nipples? Breast feeding seemed to de-sensitise my boobs. I've never really enjoyed having them handled since. But a tantalising tickle behind the knees works wonders.' Ian, too, is a convert to knee caressing. 'We happened upon knees by accident. I suppose we were en route to inner thighs at the time. We didn't get round to working our way up. Knees turned out to be well worth lingering over.'

NASAL NO-NO

Was no one going to speak up for noses? Fortunately not. We Britishers, snuffling as a nation from regular skirmishes with the common cold, tend to associate nostrils with Kleenex and Vick's Sinex. Not much room for erotica there. I did speak, though, to one man who could only experience orgasm if his shoulders were being massaged. But that's another story.

Just to make sure you don't get bogged down in the bodily back streets without an A–Z. There are more important things afoot than squandering valuable time on no-go areas like heels, or thumb nails, after all – let me direct you straight to my, purely personal, list of suggested good bits. Proceed to (1) Nape of the neck (2) Eyelids (3) Crook of the elbow (4) Belly button (5) This is still the ultimate. I'm with Ferg, Dave and Madonna. Put your best foot forward.

‍🍓28🍓

The Case For Faking It

Remember the legendary deli scene in *When Harry Met Sally*? Meg Ryan faked a double-decker megawatt multiple orgasm before demurely polishing off her pastrami on rye. Feminists in audiences the world over tsk-tsked into their popcorn. 'Antedeluvian!' 'Grotesque massaging of the chauvinist ego!' barked the outraged sisterhood. Sorry sorority, speaking as a long-term simulator, I beg to differ.

It all boils down to plain, old-fashioned politeness really. Let's assume, just for instance, that the chap ardently wielding his willy in and out of your nether regions is someone you actually rather like. Let's say, you genuinely entertain a soupçon of regard for the fellow whose testicles are swaying rhythmically only inches from the tip of your nose. Reared, as you undoubtedly were, on Anna Raeburn, Claire Rayner and sneaked snoops at your older brother's stash of *Men Only*s, you weren't exactly reticent about presenting him with a xeroxed guide to your erogenous zones. Sixties women compiled birth plans stating: I do not want my pubic hair shaved; I do not want an enema; I do not want pethidine; I wish to give birth naturally, on a bean bag, in the squatting position, without episiotomy. Nineties women compile sex plans stating:

rotate tongue clockwise around nipples; lick my armpits; digital stimulation of clitoris required; optimum inter- course-opportunity post cunnilingus; seven minutes mini- mum fornication span.

Communication is supposed to be the key to ecstasy. Experts assure us that an 'up and over' Eddie Waring-style commentary along the lines of 'not there, there' and 'harder, not that hard, higher, yeah, sling your leg over the dishwasher' will clear the air of confusion and catapult us all towards shuddering climaxes. Not a bit of it. Sex is an inexact science. You can't bonk by numbers. Despite the barrage of bulletins, compasses and diagrams you've dis- tributed and even with the best will in the world, your lover can't hit the jackpot every time.

Give the guy a break. His buttocks have been pumping like pistons. He devoted a full ten minutes to planting feathery butterfly kisses with his eyelashes behind your left kneecap just where you like it. He massaged a spoonful of Ambrosia Creamed Rice into you labia minorae. Then he licked it off again. He even remembered to take his weight on his forearms to maximise his penetrative impact. Is it his fault then that, seconds before the crucial explosion, a vivid picture of your one-year-old's nappy rash, coupled with a long-forgotten recipe for ratatouille set up camp in your brain and wouldn't be dislodged? Is it his fault you suddenly remembered it's the fifth anniversary of your last cervical smear? Is it his fault you're irretrievably off the boil?

Imagine your lover had spent all afternoon closetted in the kitchen, concocting the ultimate spag bol as a testa- ment of his love for you. Imagine that as he tremulously raised the spoon to your lips, eyes bright with anticipation of your pleasure, the acrid taste of green peppers which you've loathed with a passion ever since they cropped up with revolting regularity in school dinners deluges your taste buds. Do you gag, spit the revolting stuff into the waste disposal and splutter 'Ugh! Pukesville-city!'? Not if you've been properly brought up you don't.

My Mother says however vomit-worthy the food your hostess serves, you should acknowledge her effort and free her from embarrassment by eating at least half your portion with every appearance of enjoyment. My Mother is, as usual, absolutely right. There are times when compassion decrees it's nothing less than barbed bitchiness to be completely honest. Let the so-called sexperts sound off ad infinitum about putting your cards on the table and making clean breasts of things. Too much truth can decimate the libido irreversibly.

If your partner's given you his sexual all, isn't it pretty picky and a touch pusillanimous to lie there, distinguishable from the duvet only by your toe-nails, silently sending out the adjective 'failure'. Wouldn't it be altogether kinder, sweeter and more vivaciously in the mood of the proceedings to take a few deep juddering breaths, gasp a bit, tremble as if gripped by rippling spasms, rake his shoulders with your finger nails, groan 'Yes, yes', 'Take me, take me', or something of that ilk and at least show some team spirit?

There's nothing in this world more wretched than a tentative, 'How was it for you?' expecting the answer 'Lousy!' For goodness sake, he's the man you love and he's done his darndest to make you happy. Don't fall into the sterile sexual stranglehold which makes him feel every lovemaking is performance and you're the judge and jury, poised to produce two placards from the bedside table. Effort: 8. Orgasm: Nil.

Unfortunately, nineties lovers are conditioned to calculate their skill on a climaxes generated basis. Tell them it doesn't matter, you didn't come, but you quite enjoyed it anyway and they feel crushed beyond belief. Cuddling aptitude counts for nothing. Swoon-inducing kissing scores zilch on the Big O clapometer. That's why regular and judicious faking is essential sexual technique. It ensures that mechanical snarl-ups don't massacre a harmonious relationship. Manners are all about making other people feel comfortable. If a few seconds of writhing and 'Oh, Oh, Oh-ing' will do it, how can you be churlish enough to abstain?

Before you call me a lying doormat and disgrace to the name of liberated womanhood, let me stipulate:

1 If he's a cack-handed, blunderbuss-cocked, lazy lover, don't waste your energies faking it. Selfishness is a hopeless trait in a bed-mate. Men who aren't even trying to get it right don't deserve to be dissembled to. Tell them the truth. Their screwing sucks.

2 If he's making a prodigious effort, but you still never reach orgasm, faking is no solution. I only advocate it in the case of occasional orgasmic blips. Permanent anorgasmia probably needs professional advice to sort it out.

...blip blip blip bli

ORGASM DETECTOR

3 Never fake it on the first night. I know you're nervous and it seems like a good idea to go with the flow, but if he thinks you adore a two minute tussle in the missionary position, he'll keep dishing up more of the same and you'll have only yourself to thank.

Reserve your deceit for a man who deserves it. Lie with the one you lie with. What harm? If he feels confident enough about himself to relax, who knows, you might be acting a whole lot less and coming massively more?

The great pretenders

There's no telling how many women fake orgasm, or how often, but in one recent magazine survey of more than 40,000 American women, forty-six per cent admitted they fake it – eight per cent frequently, or always. In another, seventy per cent of women and ninety-eight per cent of men said they usually or always have an orgasm. But forty-eight per cent of those interviewed – predominantly women – said they sometimes pretend to come. Meanwhile, an anonymous poll of twenty-one working women in New York City found that sixty-two per cent admitted to having faked it at least once – regardless of age and marital status.

How to win a faking-it oscar

1 Moan. Very important to get the tone right. There are certain women who's favourite moan is: 'I want to go to Marbella'. This is inappropriate here. The ideal moan is a mixture of just-caught-my-finger-in-the-car-door and, God? You're here for dinner? Tonight? I thought we said NEXT Thursday. The pain/surprise combo is unbeatable for simulated ecstasy.
2 Groan. Use constipation/childbirth as your sound-alike role model. Grit teeth. Tense chin. And let rip.
3 Heavy Breathing. N.B. Through the MOUTH, not the NOSE. You don't want to be snorting all over the poor

fellow. Keep a brown paper bag by the bed to put over your head in case of hyperventilation. (In some cases, brown paper bags over both partners' head DURING sex (nostril holes strategically pierced) can be a substantial *aide-fantasie*.)

4 Bucking and writhing, more aerobically known as 'sit-ups'. This has fringe benefits. It's an excellent waist-line firming exercise. Average four bucks per minute for maximum toning results.

5 Twitching vaginal muscles. Yours should be strong enough to hold a drinking straw up there. Why? Don't ask me.

6 Collapsing as if spent. Very restful. With time you will appear so acutely spent, he has to get up and make the tea.

Can he tell?

Men may delude themselves they can tell if their partner has had an orgasm, but they haven't a prayer. According to The Kinsey Institute New Report On Sex, there's no way a man can swear an affidavit that you've climaxed, short of wiring you to equipment that measures blood pressure, heart rate, vaginal contractions, brain activity, etc. Just our luck Dixons probably have Orgasm-Detector Machines planned for general release this Summer, price £17.99.

✨29✨

Even Your Subconscious is Knackered - You Dream About Trains Hurtling Through Tunnels And You're Really Talking British Rail!

So there I was, nipples akimbo, bouncing on a Beverly Hills water-bed while Kurt Russell lapped gently at my labia, the Coldstream Guards marched past playing 'Matchmaker, matchmaker' and a pink elephant in flamenco gear flew through the palm trees. Everything was going swimmingly until, goddammit, I woke up next to snoring husband in boring NW10.

Some of the best sex I've never had used to happen when I was asleep. And with some of the hunkiest beefcakes I've never slept with too. In all modesty, my subconscious used to be a wow! I spent my twenties blushing while they weighed my courgettes at Waitrose, as the memory of my full frontal frolics with Fred Flintstone and the London Symphony Orchestra the night before, surged embarrassingly into my brain. Bed used to be a blast. If I wasn't doing it, I was dreaming it. These days, though, my dreams are only after one thing – a decent night's kip.

I'm not kidding. My subconscious is shot to hell. And

I'm not the only one. Every former dream sex maniac I know has been reduced to pathetically tame Neighbours meets Blue Peter snippets and vintage driving towards a cliff edge in a brakeless Honda nightmares. Danielle put it down to having three children aged two, four and six and a chronically disrupted sleep pattern. 'Jesus, after bathing and bedding the children and breastfeeding my husband, I haven't the energy for dreaming. If I can snatch a few hours' rest I'm eternally grateful. Sexual high jinks at the same time is just too exhausting to contemplate.'

Why are our subconsciouses U-rated shadows of their former selves?

1 **Pregnancy:** getting up seventeen times a night to pass a thimbleful of urine sends the subconscious a signal. 'Futile mate. Save your energies. Don't squander your best group grope/Lesbian lilo love-ins or caviar wrestling dreams on this one.' Overnight your torrid nocturnal knocking shop becomes distressingly chaste. Pre-pregnancy we're talking Superman, minus the tights. During, you're lucky if Jack and Jill make it up the hill without a chaperone.

2 **Parenthood:** this divides unpleasantly into three insomniac stages.

i *Baby*

Babies don't give a burp about dream patterns. They claim not to know they're supposed to subside into somnolence at 6.30 prompt, and not wake up till 7.30 (9.30 on Sundays). Child-centric society be damned! Babies are sadistic little blighters, chin-deep in original sin. They get their kicks pooing and yelling at unsociable hours. Experts claim new parents sleep, sporadically, in six minute bursts. Do not believe them. The hideous truth is that new parents never sleep at all. Don't be fooled by appearances. A parent-nouveau reclining with closed eyelids is never asleep. A prostrate parent-nouveau with sealed lids is only ever doing one thing. Praying. 'Praying for what?' I hear you ask. Praying to fall asleep long enough to wake up and find out this shocking playing mummies and daddies experience is all a bad dream, that's what. Nouveaux parents will confirm that they are too tired to be subconscious.

ii   *Toddler*

All toddlers must be bought extortionately expensive 'big boy's/girl's beds'. These are essential to give a child something to climb out of, burst into the parental boudoir and say: 'Let Daddy sleep in my hand-painted, Thomas the Tank Engine bed, Mummy. There are fat, greasy chicken-sausage monsters underneath it. I'll sleep with you.' As this is the eighth such intrusion in two hours, parents have no choice but to capitulate.

DAD'S FATE

Spitting obscenities, Dad decamps to Junior's child-sized bed and attempts to fold himself into a four-year-old's foetal position. Several yards of paternal extremity dangle, glacially over the edge of Junior's Fireman Sam duvet. On closer inspection, the sticky object now embedded in Dad's ear turns out to be a half-sucked barley sugar. Dad dreams he is Alice in Wonderland as the caterpillar says: 'One side will make you grow smaller. The other will make you grow taller.' Dad usually only has dreams starring white rabbits after nights of awesomely inebriated debauchery. This makes him feel even worse.

MUM'S FATE

FACT: Toddlers on television commercials sleep the rosy, petal-soft sleep of Boucher cherubs.

FACT: Toddlers who've invaded the marital bed snore, fart and swarm. 'Huh!' I hear you say. 'A likely story. How can one tiny, precious, innocent toddler possibly be said to swarm?' Because, as survivors will confirm, sharing sheets with a toddler is indistinguishable from bunking-up with a swarm of locusts/bees/traffic wardens. They flail disconcertingly from pillow to post, pausing only to biff you in the head with their teddies. At five minute intervals they prise your eyelids open and say: 'Mummy, me want eat toffee, wear swimming trunks and armbands and watch Sooty and Sweep video?' By 4.15 a.m. his baby teeth are rotting quietly, the armbands are inflated, Matthew Corbett's swapping sweet nothings with Soo, and Mum is composing her letter to VSO.

iii *Teenage*

When there's nothing important for them to stay awake for, children, despite drugs, violence and bribery, refuse to sleep. The moment you actually want them to wake up, do their chemistry revision, mow the lawn, forge their futures, amount to something, they become unrousable. Babes don't sleep the sleep of babes. Teenagers do. Aim a Hoover on full power right at a sleeping teenage head, and I guarantee not a blackhead will stir, not a nose-ring flicker. 'Fine,' I hear you say, 'plenty of time for Ma and Pa to catch up on some shut-eye.' 'Not so fast,' I reply. Teenagers, like marsupials, awaken just as their parents are changing into their winceyette, stick their heads round the bedroom door and say: 'Bye.' 'Bye? What the hell do you mean, Bye? It's 11.35. Where the **** can you possibly be ****ing going

BUT WHAT DO DREAMS REALLY MEAN?

DREAM I was eating a large, ripe banana.

MEANING There's no fruit in the house. The children will contract scurvy and rickets and you'll never be able to show your face on the telly again.

DREAM I was climbing up the Eiffel Tower.

MEANING The light fittings are all dusty. For God's sake, get the kitchen step ladder out and giving them a going over with Mr Muscle.

DREAM I was on a train, hurtling down a long, dark tunnel.

MEANING I'm definitely in two minds about the privatisation of British Rail.

DREAM I kept biting the heads off cucumbers.

MEANING The vegetable patch wants mulching.

at 11 ****ing 35?' The answer is always identical: 'Out!'

This leaves parents' thoughts free to roam unfettered along the following avenues:

- fatal car crashes
- police-busted raves
- fast women
- fast food
- dens of iniquity

Naturally, the parent of teenagers sacrifices his/her subconscious on the altar of worry.

WET DREAMS

We all know about adolescent boys and their wet dreams. In reality, the medically termed 'nocturnal emissions' continue to plague many men well into their mid-life crises. Did you know sticky pyjamas have a female equivalent. Apparently women have wet, or should I say moist dreams too. Some grown women, without hand to genital contact, without any physical stimulation whatsoever, experience stupendous orgasms in their sleep. I should be so lucky.

178

❤30❤

Orgasmic Etiquette

Aching to send Virginia Bottomley an enema, but unsure how to address the envelope? Tempted to tackle cherries in public, but floundering on the pip front? Frightened of a debilitating fish-fork *faux pas*? No problem. Debrett's and a host of expert etiquetters are on hand to lead you through the social minefield of fingerbowls and serviette origami unscathed. Don't know how to duck out of a dinner-party invitation without causing offence? Worry not, they have the answers. Don't know how to duck out of oral sex without offending your spouse? You're strictly on your own baby. Have you noticed, etiquette expertise stops outside the bedroom door? We're bombarded with advice on colour/fabric/ brand of sheets (white Egyptian cotton, anything else is strictly *de trop*), but when it comes to advice on what goes on between them – zilcho.

I, for one, would appreciate a modicum of guidance. Let's face it, sex can be a social nightmare. Embarrassing? Of course it is. Even between long-term loving partners? Are you kidding? John Lydon of the Sex Pistols described sex as 'two minutes, fifty two seconds of squishing noises'. I only wish it was that simple.

Q: My husband leaves his socks on in bed. Is this a social gaffe?

A: Only if the socks are white.

Q: Is it non-u to leave the TV on during sex?

A: Wildlife programmes on BBC 2 are both acceptable and encouraging.

Q: My wife likes to beat me with a spatula while listening to Bruce Springsteen. Is this lower middle-class?

A: Beating is fine. Bruce is fine. Lose the spatula. Too downmarket. Substitute something sharp by Sabatier.

Q: I've just found out my lover is Catholic, but I'd still like him to sip soup from my temple of delight. Will he be offended?

A: Not if you make it bouillabaisse on Fridays.

Q: Who goes on top?

A: Whoever gets there first.

> Please note: shouting, 'Hey Hon, slip off and let me sit astride willya!' lacks finesse. If you're unhappy with the bottom bunk, it is quite acceptable to attempt a mid-thrust flip. OK somersaulting fourteen stones of indelible bulk isn't easy. But who said good sex was? Naturally, it might slide out and the two of you end up on the shagpile in a mottled heap. Be that as it may, the hint has been given.

Q: What if (s)he's rubbing against the wrong bit?

A: With practice, your bedroom will sound like a conference of on-duty traffic cops. 'Up! Down! Hang a right!' Important terms of endearments for the nineties! Relish every bossy moment. After all, you wouldn't dare talk to the guy who installed your

PRACTICAL TIP

My friends Deborah and Martin flip a coin for who's on top. Talk about an organised household!

kitchen units like that. If you did, he'd down tools and be out of there in a flash of Nike.

Q: That's all very well, but how do I get him/her to do it right?

A: Unfortunately lovers are not vibrators. They're infinitely less efficient. And they're subject to troublesome things called 'feelings'. If you've chosen flesh over plastic, sex isn't entirely performance related. Pick up a catalogue and find something sleek, black and batteried that won't need a cup of tea afterwards.

Q: Do I spit or swallow?

A: That depends. You should have been paying attention in Chapters 5 and 6.

Q: What if he wilts unwontedly?

A: Pretending it's fine and dandy and you weren't really all that keen on climaxing anyway is pretty useless. If you'd wanted to dig over the compost heap, what on earth were you having sex for?

Q: So what do I do then, smartarse?

A: Take up a musical instrument.

Q: How does one react to a fanny fart?

A: The etiquette situation is elementary. If a friend breaks wind at a restaurant during the soup course, you crack loud, insensitive, boorish jokes about it. So does every other eater at the table. The same applies in bed.

Q: Should I talk dirty?

A: One man's dirt is another woman's Ajax Lemon Liquid. Problems arise when your partner insists on whispering extremely tame drivellings about Roseanne and Key Lime Pie into your shell-like, and you're desperate for some filthy smut. In my opinion, what you have in mind for Keanu Reeves, a Smurf and a tube of Macleans is no-one's business but your own.

PRACTICAL TIP

In extreme circumstances Walkman wearing is permissible.

How to conduct yourself in extremis

My Mother says you never really know a man until you've heard him drink soup. Many a Cecil Gee suit conceals a suit-spraying slurper. My Auntie Carole, on the other hand, claims you've never really fathomed a chap till you've shared sanitary ware. Does he leave the lid up? Worse still, does he leave it down, bedewed with dribbles? Are there stubble scrapings in the basin and pubic outcrops in the soap? Does he abuse your Crabtree & Evelyn Body Lotion? Is he an immaculate towel folder, or a remorseless towel dropper? 'Asinine idiocy!' say I. There's only one fail-safe method of measuring your man's mettle. Stop thinking of Benidorm and concentrate. How does he conduct himself mid-come?

No doubt about it, the Big O is a great leveller. Smooth talkers can be crass climaxers. Talk about making a grown man cry! There's nothing quite like satisfactory tube-emptying to turn a macho brute into a snivelling sissy. The disturbing thing about climactic behaviour is its unpredictability. Ecstasy does funny things to fellas. Granted, we women are prone to a spot of panting, the odd 'Aaaah!' or even 'Oooh!' not to mention the ever-popular 'Yes! Yes!' Males, however, definitely take the orgasmic biscuit. How do menfolk express themselves in the throes of earthly bliss. Here are the results of a recent cosmic survey in order of popularity.

1   Sobbing – varies between the three Kleenex variety and the quiet sniffle. Can be a bit of a downer for the sobbee.
2   Howling and whooping – not so much Kevin Costner, more the wolves.
3   Yodelling – has a certain Alpine freshness, unsuitable

for semi/terraced/apartment-dwellers with impressionable neighbours.

4 Barking – can't you just smell the Prime Pal with rich marrowbone?

5 Total earth shattering silence.

The problem with 5, the strong silent type, is there's always the probability he may have dropped dead. Remember Goldie Hawn's first husband in *Private Benjamin*? Remember the Reagans' chum, New York magnate Alfred Bloomingdale? Both popped their clogs in the nicest possible way. Call me old fashioned, but ever since my husband's thirty-fifth birthday, I can't get them out of my mind. Quiet comings freak me out. I'm practically dialling 999 on the mobile.

That said, I do find the wailers, screamers and woof-woofs a trifle off putting. Less so, however, than the pillow biters, neck gnawers and bed-head shakers. With special mention to the chaps who can't quite climax without raking your back with their nails.

Naturally if you happen to be a thumb-sucking sheet-chewer with yodelling tendencies yourself, finding a compatible comer won't pose a problem. My ideal is a melodious breather who clasps my buttocks adoringly at the crucial moment. Which reminds me:

Q: Is it polite to come before (s)he does?
A: Ladies first doesn't apply on the orgasm stakes. These days it's dog eat dog up there. Do yourself a favour and take it when you can get it.
Q: Who gets up for the wodge of tissues?
A: If you haven't learned to keep them on your bedside table by now, serves you right if you catch your death darting to the sub-zero bathroom, starkers.

❦ 31 ❦

How Not To - Gracefully

The world is cowering under an unstoppable scourge of 'How To' books. Agents, authors and publishers uniformly work on the assumption that we're NOT, but we WOULD if only we knew HOW. Would what? Any subversive bloody activity they can invent to plague us. We're talking 'How To': Bond With Your Bowel/Bring Out The Pussy-Cat In Your Doberman/Create Paint Effects With Suppositories/Master DIY Plastic Surgery/Earn A Living With Your Teeth. Every 'How To' book is a deeply personal accusation. It's not publishing, it's commodities broking. The (consistently lucrative) commodity is our insecurity. That's why there's always a soft-focus smug mug on the shiny jacket, smirking cat-with-the-creamishly from a home-upholstered chaise-longue. The message is inescapable. 'THIS IS AN IMPROVING BOOK. AND, BOY, DO YOU NEED IMPROVING. I CAN LOSE FIVE STONE ON THE TERMINAL DISEASE DIET/RE-TILE MY ROOF USING OLD EGG BOXES/SHAG THE ENTIRE BOARD OF AN INTERNATIONAL CORPORATION, AND YOU CAN'T.' We are all heart-breakingly, pathetically, hopelessly eager to be improved. Tell us we're frigid sloths with suet thighs, shocking ball-sense and horrible curtains and we lap it up. No matter that we didn't even specially want to 'Breed

Herring In The En Suite Bathroom'. The knowledge that someone else is making obscene amounts of money flogging a book about it is enough to have us scrabbling for our credit cards.

Of course, we don't actually READ these books. They're the literary equivalent of exercise bicycles or Milk of Magnesia. Owning them is sufficient. Using them would be gilding the lily. This means, none of us ever knows 'How To' anything whatsoever, but we do know we need to know and we've put our money where our faults are. Of course, the truth is we haven't the slightest intention of learning 'How To' because we're perfectly happy watching Noel's House Party. What we badly need to know is 'How NOT To'. After all, just think of all the things you are NOT doing right now. You are NOT, for example, Rearing Rodents The Spiritual Way, Constructing Your Own Cornflake Scale Model of Leeds Castle or even Learning To Appreciate Shakespeare in Esperanto. The point is are you NOT doing these things to the best of your ability? Be honest with yourself: you are an untutored non-doer. Every day there are a billion and one things you're NOT doing in total, shaming ignorance of the best possible optimum way NOT to do them. There is, if publishers would but realise it, an enormous gap in the market. An uncharted area where all we're aching for guidance. How, in the name of progress, will we ever get the hang of NOT doing things supremely well, if no-one brings out definitive volumes explaining, in words of one syllable, with copious glossy colour illustrations, HOW NOT TO do them? Wouldn't you dash straight out and plonk down piles of steaming readies for: 'How Not To Tune Into Karmic Astrology' and 'How Not To Turn Old T-Shirts Into Patchwork Quilts'? I know I would.

Why don't they clear a space next to all those *How To Have Supersonic Sex* books, and tell us long-monogs what we really want to know: how not to – gracefully. I mean, the headache's been done to death, and a girl can't have the time of the month for more than six weeks solid without seeing a gynaecologist. We're in dire need of innovative, yet sensitive ways to wriggle out of it without naffing him off good and proper. And, let's not subside into arrant sexism here. The urge to NOT is far from all one way traffic. Many's the time a man doesn't remotely feel like doing what a man's gotta do. How does he disentangle his recumbent winkle from the persistent pummellings of his voracious partner without leaving her rejected and seething? Logically speaking, there's no reason why our horny moments should ever coincide.

Scenario 1

Him

Stimulating day at work including:

a   generously proportioned promotion
b   generously proportioned temporary secretary
c   generously proportioned expense account lunch followed by
d   generously proportioned relax with the paper
e   generously proportioned supper prepared by wife

RESULT:
Hard, hot and horny as hell.

Her

Shitty day at work including:

a   dropping snotty child off at snotty child-minder
b   dropping unfinished work off at snotty printer
c   dropping Boots cottage cheese bap on best jacket
    followed by
d   dropping washing in machine, snotty child in bath
e   dropping spag bol into gaping mouths of snotty child
    and snotty husband

RESULT:

Wouldn't if you goddam paid her.

Scenario 2

Him

Stinking Saturday at home including:

a   unbunging sink
b   unbunging drains
c   unbunging nose of snotty child followed by
d   unbunging strange, rattly noise coming from dish-
    washer
e   unbunging rear of constipated, snotty child

RESULT:

Would hang himself by the bollocks first.

Her

Rapturous Saturday out including:

a   picking up a cluster of old girlfriends

TIMES WHEN YOUR REQUIREMENTS ARE UNLIKELY TO COINCIDE

- Mondays
- Tuesdays
- Wednesdays
- Thursdays
- Fridays
- Saturdays
- Sundays

TIMES WHEN YOUR REQUIREMENTS ARE LIKELY TO COINCIDE

- holidays
- birthdays
- after inappropriate consumption of alcohol
- when you win the National Lottery

b   picking up an amusing Georgian back-scratcher

c   picking up suggestive glances from a disreputable Frenchman followed by

d   picking up a couple of nifty little jackets

e   picking up a Chinese takeaway

RESULT:
Majorly primed to get down on it.

So, you'd rather pumice the hard skin off your feet, and your partner's advancing optimistically with a predatory look glinting in both rampant eyes. How do you extricate yourself from an unwelcome conjugal embrace without rocking the marriage right down to its already pretty ropey foundations?

The Feltz guide to how not to – gracefully

Don't give way to cliché
Never have:

1   a headache
2   women's troubles
3   a slipped disc

You owe it to your partner to stump up something a touch more imaginative.

Avoid at all costs
I know these phrases are tempting. I know they're on the tip of your tongue. I know they are also all:

a   true
b   succinct

188

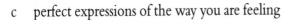

c   perfect expressions of the way you are feeling

BUT they will not do your chances of living happily ever after any favours. In response to a request for a bit of nookie, NEVER SAY:

- 'God, no!'
- 'Sod off, we only did it last Friday.'
- 'Ask your Mother. You seem to think she's so brilliant at everything else!'
- 'I'd rather have a hysterectomy.'
- 'What do you think I am, a masochist?'
- 'See you in hell first, Beer-gut.'
- 'You must be joking.'
- 'Try the au pair.'

How not to – gracefully – for men

I may be drummed out of the Brownies for saying this, but all women are suckers for cuddles. This includes dungaree wearers. Deflect unwanted overtures by saying (preferably in love-laden tones), and definitely in your own words, something along the lines of: 'Darling, sex we can have any time. Tonight I just want to be close to you. Hold you in my arms. Inhale the fragrance of your hair. Cuddle you against my heart till morning.' I guarantee lurrve will kick in, and lust fly right out the double glazing.

How not to – gracefully – for women

This is a toughie. I've spent many years cogitating on this theme and have come to the conclusion that men don't care if:

a   you've broken a nail
b   you've broken a leg
c   you've broken your waters

They still want sex

There's no point presenting them with cogently argued Socratic rhetoric arguing the case against having sex because their hard-ons (or is it hards-on) don't respond to reason.

This works for me (sometimes)

I'm not at all sure about the morality of this, but it's one I've used at home with varying degrees of success for the past nine years. If you get the feeling he might be on the cusp of initiating carnal proceedings, hurry up and take – or PRETEND to take – a sleeping pill. Yawn ostentatiously. Curl into uncurlable ball. Drift – quickly, speed is of the essence – into a deep, satisfying and utterly unrousable sleep. Remain unrousable. Should he attempt, even minor physical contact, snore, utter a stream of incomprehensible sleep-talk, and roll out of arm's reach.

N.B. Used judiciously this is a winner because:

a   most men don't have the heart to wake, much less penetrate, a deeply slumbering spouse
b   you haven't actually said or done anything to reject him. It wasn't your fault you were dead to the world when he finally got his act together.

Caution

Do not over use. This technique pales with repetition.

Going Through Condoms

🍓32🍓

Contraceptives Work By Putting Us Off Sex (Or, Do You Fancy A Mouthful of Spermicide?)

If we're not Catholics or Orthodox Jews, we're expected to genuflect daily before the Almighty to thank him for the heavenly, hedonistic gift of contraception. Contraceptives are all things bright and beautiful. All the high jinks without any of the responsibility. All the pokes without any of the procreation. Double your pleasure, double your fun. The key to domestic bacchanalia.

Balderdash! Show me a pre-menopausal woman and I'll show you someone with an atrophied cap, dangling coil, ruptured sponge, pill allergy and a husband who says: 'Real men don't use rubbers. It's like having a shower with your raincoat on.'

The pill

Thirty years ago, the contraceptive pill was hailed as the mighty liberator of womankind. Now it's known as the mighty liberator of:

1   spots
2   swollen breasts
3   weight gain
4   migraine
5   thrombosis
6   nausea
7   fatigue
8   mood swings

and, supreme irony of ironies,

9   loss of libido!!!!!!!

It's true that if you take the pill regularly you won't get pregnant – barring diarrhoea and interaction with certain antibiotics. It's also true that if you take the pill regularly you won't feel like trying. What's more, given that the average couple copulates twice a week, is there really any point having twenty-four-hour contraceptive cover? What's even more, the definitive results of the original case studies begun in the sixties still haven't hit the fan. So, you might just be giving yourself zits, clots, fat and a foul temper and something a hell of a lot more unpleasant, like early death, for example, besides.

N.B. Thousands of women who have no problem fathoming Einstein's Theory Of Relativity persist in subscribing to the vain hope that if you forget your pill for a couple of days, you simply knock back three pills on the third day. Wrong! A packet of half popped pills in the dresser drawer may LOOK contraceptive, but if you ain't eaten them, they ain't on duty.

The coil

The coil is a pig of a contraceptive. It hurts like stink to get it in. It hurts like expletive deleted to yank it out. It magnifies the menstrual period into a Steven Spielberg special effect. Oceanic haemorrhages and pain that makes natural childbirth feel like minor discomfort are fringe benefits of the coil. If you spot a grown woman turn alabaster, clutch her stomach and slide gracefully down the wall at Sainsbury's, you'll know she's a coil wearer. Like Sandy Shaw's puppet, coil's come on a string. Unlike Sandy Shaw's puppet, most averagely endowed men can feel the string waggling when they make love. Making penile contact with a waggling string is at best disconcerting, at worst a terminal anti-aphrodisiac.

If, despite my lurid efforts, you feel yourself inclining towards a coil, be warned. Many a bouncing nine pounder has made its entrance into the world with its infant fist curled picturesquely around a pristine coil. In short, the coil doesn't always work. So you might as well bypass the torrential periods, agonising stomach cramps, undignified string quartet and get pregnant the pleasant way.

The cap

No-one refers to the Cantonese pill, or the Albanian coil, but the cap is always Dutch. No matter if it's made in Hong Kong, bought in Birmingham and used by an Asian in Midlothian, that cap remains Dutch. Don't be fooled by the nomenclature. The Dutch cap is not to be confused with clogs, tulips, Rembrandt, red light districts or any of that other heart-warming Walloon-Flemish heritage.

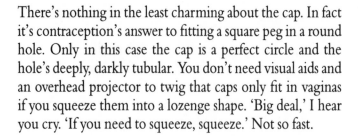

🍓 Going Through Condoms

As my GP sweetly said: 'The cap's an excellent form of contraception, if you don't mind getting pregnant.'

Note: Caps need servicing as regularly as motors. Otherwise, one thrust and you've got atrophied rubber and an extra mouth to feed.

There's nothing in the least charming about the cap. In fact it's contraception's answer to fitting a square peg in a round hole. Only in this case the cap is a perfect circle and the hole's deeply, darkly tubular. You don't need visual aids and an overhead projector to twig that caps only fit in vaginas if you squeeze them into a lozenge shape. 'Big deal,' I hear you cry. 'If you need to squeeze, squeeze.' Not so fast.

A RIDDLE

When is a cap not a cap? Not when it's ajar. That's a door, you pillock. A cap is not a cap *sans* spermicide. Spermicide is an odious ointment guaranteeing seminal genocide which must be squirted in generous dollops all over the cap. Naturally, when you attempt to squeeze the cap into the necessary lozenge shape, one handed because the other hand's busy parting your labia minorae, it whooshes out of your grasp like a lubricated UFO and sticks fast to the ceiling, a shrunken and embarrassing frisbee.

IT GETS WORSE

Anyone hungover enough to mistake spermicide for toothpaste will confirm the following:

1   Dutch caps and cunnilingus are mutually exclusive
2   Any idiot attempting to combine them will be stricken dumb for up to a month as the spermicide commences fatal bombardment of his tongue cells

AND WORSE

Not only do you have to insert a cap ... prior to intercourse, thereby

a   eradicating spontaneity
b   making you feel like a pre-meditative nymphomaniac

you also have to leave the whole squelchy, spermy mess up there for a minimum of six hours after the event. No use bathing, bideting, or scented intimate towelling with the loathsome object still inside. As if that weren't enough, the cap is notoriously unreliable.

The female condom

At last it's my turn to malign the Femidom. Yippee! I know every alternative comedian in the land has had a bash, but this is my book and I demand my turn. I was berserk about those Femidom posters. 'Johnny's Had A Sex Change'. Brilliant! Try the female condom and I guarantee you'll also fancy a sex change. No sex at all. I'll tell you why. Unwrap it, I should say, shake it out and what do you find? Femidom looks like a Tesco carrier bag, only a slightly baggier and a bit less tailored. I'd like to know who the manufacturers used for fittings? Wookey Hole, perhaps? To give it its due, Femidom comes in extremely useful about the house. So versatile. Wheelie bin liners. Winter waterproofing for the barbeque. You name it. Having said that, insertion's no picnic. It says on the box: 'First find your cervix.' Do me a favour. Assuming you found it, how the hell would you know it was your cervix, anyway? Your head's between your legs. It's practically a re-birthing experience. In fact, you're hoping you might get lucky and finally bump into your G-spot. If you want to know what wearing a Femidom actually feels like, may I suggest stuffing your Sunday tablecloth up your right nostril.

If you read the small print closely it says: 'If Femidom is correctly inserted, participants will be entirely unaware of its presence during intercourse.' So we tried it. All I can say is, one thrust, and my husband was spread-eagled on the duvet, in agony, howling for a Bandaid, frenziedly clutching his winkle. Blow me if I hadn't left in a couple of packets of frozen turkey schnitzels!

The sponge

OK to wash your face with. Rubbish as a contraceptive. Doesn't fit snugly enough, so any enterprising sperm front-crawl it round the edges.

Depot provera injections

Vaccinations are bad enough when there's a holiday at the end of them. Faced with no nookie or the needle, I know which I'd bloody choose.

Condoms

Condoms are so trendy these days it's almost churlish to leave home without one. Nonetheless most long-monogs treat them like party manners – essential when out, but utterly unnecessary at home. Stultifying similes along the lines of: 'I'm not wearing one of those, it's like paddling with your wellies on' are common bedroom parlance. Real meaning? 'I'm prepared to sacrifice your health and happiness for the sake of my unfettered sperm, Sweetheart.'

DESIGNER JOHNNIES

A brisk trade continues in novelty condoms. Blue ones, black ones with sensitive ridges, paisley patterned ones with bows on, rag-rolled ones with *faux* marble borders. The question is, when should a woman state her preference? Let's face it, if he presents Percy togged up in psychedelic tartan, you may decide his member doesn't get your vote. As a general guideline, stick to sickly pink, it never did your Mother any harm.

IMPORTANT NEWS FLASH

They don't flush. No use trying. Two weeks later, to all intents and purposes, there's a captive jelly fish in your loo. I recommend tying a knot and wrapping it in tissues. Move quickly, though, otherwise it'll stick to the bedside table and you can expect a permanent souvenir where the veneer's come away.

The choice, as they say on infuriating low budget game shows, is yours!

♥33♥

Extracurricular Dabblings (Or, Shagging Around)

I'm the product of a traditional Jewish upbringing. To me, an affair is a wedding, a barmitzvah or, at a pinch, a circumcision. Something you buy a new hat, bag and matching shoes for.

There's always some pillock prepared to write 'My Affair Saved My Marriage' articles for women's magazines. They have to, poor sods. They need the dosh to pay their divorce lawyers. They espouse The Affair As Aphrodisiac theory. This theory is the ideal way to commit adultery without taking the flak. It's based on the premise that shagging around can be an altruistic mission to save your marriage. Here, in case you've managed to avoid it, is the thinking behind the piffle.

JOKE

Becky: Sadie, you look radiant. What's your secret?
Sadie: Becky, don't tell anyone. I'm having an affair.
Becky: Congratulations! Who's doing the catering?

1 If you're bored with sex at home, spice it up with lunch-time grapplings in obscure Holiday Inns with people whose buttocks are firmer/juicier than your husband/wife's.

2 The excitment of fumbling forbidden fruit will propel you into such a cracking libidinous renaissance that, even when faced with your husband/wife's knackered old protruberances, you'll plough in, lustily.

3 The stimulating subterfuge involved in pretending

you're working late when you're really screwing in the stationery cupboard will bring out the James Bond/ Mata Hari element that has lain dormant in your psyche all these years.

4   When you've finished being altruistic, the owner of the freshly-squeezed buttocks will trek off quietly to a new job in Newcastle taking all incriminating evidence with her/him.

Of course this is a load of tosh because:

1   If you're really having hot sex at lunchtime you'll be far too bushed to manage more than half of Coronation Street in the evening.

2   The pressure of maintaining a virtuoso sexual performance on a par with your forbidden partner will definitely bring you out in coronaries/diabetes/ prickly heat.

3   The aggravation of hiding your Access bills, de-lipsticking your collar, rinsing alien bodily fluids off your smalls and combing your pockets for suspicious bus tickets means that when the children say: 'Dad/Mum, guess what? I came top in my history test,' you growl: 'No, you bloody well cannot stay up to watch 'Sex Talk' you randy little swine.'

4   Pert-buttocked playthings are never, ever, offered conveniently far-flung jobs in Newcastle. They either (a) get promoted and become your boss, (N.B. Having a boss who has love-bitten your inner thighs is NEVER a good career move) or (b) get promoted and make sure you are exiled to Newcastle.

And above all

5   What happens when your peach-bottomed plaything turns into a person?

Secret shags are people too

Despite all that Erica Jong spiel about 'zipless fucks' humans aren't designed to fornicate without emoting. You may think you can open your legs/deposit your seed with alley-cat impunity, but some day, somewhere, one of your scalps/belt-notches will touch you, not just genitally, but emotionally. Good Lord! You thought you were an ice-cool philanderer, dispassionately consorting with a bit on the side. Suddenly, you're a love-stricken swain, composing sonnets to your darling's eyebrows. Sorry Mate, you're part of the most excruciating geometric configuration known to (wo)man – The Eternal Triangle.

This is a vile situation which never has a happy ending.

First ugly scenario

A is married to B but can't get C's incisive brain and lilac eyes out of his/her head = TERMINAL MISERY. Because either:

1   C is perfectly happy fooling around, thanks very much. C plighted his/her troth last year to the love of his/her life, Alex(andra), currently away at sea. C has every intention of marrying him/her next April and going to live in Suffolk to breed Airedales. Which leaves A devastated, bereft, snappish at home and absent-minded in meetings. Logically, of course, he can't possibly blame C, because she is the love of his life and, as such, flawless. Naturally, he takes out his wrath, frustration and the net effect of too many late night Kentucky Fried Chickens on B. B wonders at first if A

is anaemic/constipated/about to be made redundant before surmising correctly that A is having an affair.

CONCLUSION

- A is heartbroken.
- B is heartbroken.
- C is fairly pissed off.

or

2 C is absolutely bowled over by A and can't wait to whisk A away from spiritless suburbia and into a converted warehouse in Docklands with views of industrial effluent and exposed beams. C loves A. A loves C. A and C eat a great many insalata tricolores at expensive restaurants in the Fulham Road convincing themselves that B will be far better off without A in the long run. Once they have definitively proved they are only doing it as a favour to B, A tells B fifteen years, two mortgages, three kids and a hamster have been (i) suffocating (ii) intellectual suicide and (iii) a farce. A leaves B to join C who is waiting in a nippy two-seater.

CONCLUSION

- A is momentarily elated, but ultimately garroted by alimony, unavoidable access to three belligerent teen-agers every Sunday, and C's incessant demands for sex.
- B is heartbroken.
- C is momentarily elated, but ultimately hacked off by A's children/alimony/feeble sex drive.

Second ugly scenario

A is married to B while contentedly shagging C. C has had it with mopping up B's left-overs and is determined to secure the presence of A at Xmas and public holidays as well as between 8.17 and 9.36 on Thursday nights = TERMINAL MISERY because:

> A can hardly remember C's name, let alone whether C takes sugar and has no intention whatsoever of breaking up the happy home/falling out with wealthy in-laws/facing the music for C's sake. When A told C repeatedly that A loved C more than the grains of sand in the Sahara, A, quite obviously, didn't mean a word of it. A was simply succumbing to conventional extra-curricular dabbling parlance. C should have been adult enough to realise the flowers, chocolates and fluffy stuffed kittens were not love tokens, but shag-on-the-side tokens. A is sure C will act like an adult/see sense.
>
> Sense, to C, means ringing B and spewing forth unsavoury details of A and C's most uninhibited couplings. It also means faxing declarations of love to A's office at times of the day when at least seventeen of A's colleagues are guaranteed to read them. Not to mention threatening (i) suicide (ii) violence (iii) nervous breakdown.

CONCLUSION

- A is terrified.
- B is heartbroken.
- C is humiliated beyond belief.

Temptation, temptation, temptation

Lest you call me a sanctimonious prig, let me hasten to add, affairs are extremely easy to resist, if no-one's offering. It's when a real, flesh and blood – and fanciable flesh and blood at that – human being, with whom you have NOT been dental flossing every night for a decade, actually shows an interest that resisting gets a mite tougher. It goes without saying, on principle, none of us would countenance adultery. It's only when principles become people we start compromising them.

Only long-monogs know how overwhelmingly terrif it is to be seduced after years of being taken for granted. You're used to 'How about it, then?' or 'OK, but pull my nightie down when you've finished.' Suddenly you're being treated to: 'It's remarkable the way the sun brings out the copper lights in your hair' and you melt from the eyeballs downwards. The contrast is just too great. Every inch of your underappreciated being responds to your seducer. Of course you know it's wrong. You're perfectly well aware you shouldn't even chance a clandestine chop suey. But there's an unaccustomed turmoil stirring 'neath your knickers, adrenalin's gushing into every extremity, you haven't felt so friskily youthful for yonks, and besides:

a   you've only got one life
b   a few bamboo shoots never did anyone any harm
c   no-one will ever know

Now that's where you're wrong. Because:

a   One life can seem like a life sentence when your seducer was only after a brisk shafting and now:
   i   your spouse is grievously wounded

ii   your kids are in tatters

iii you're washed up in a one-bedroom cess-pit, branded a Baddie

b   Clandestine bamboo shoots are always the preamble to clandestine coitus. Otherwise you could happily invite your partner along.

c   Someone always finds out. If you don't believe me, ask Sir Peter Harding.

Epilogue

🍓34🍓

Whys and Wherefores

Philip Larkin wrote: 'Sexual intercourse began in 1963.'

I was born in 1962, which only goes to prove I come from pioneering stock. Three decades may have passed since then, but sexual hypocrisy is still rampant. In this day and AIDS, sexual honesty has never been more vital. Yet we continue to subscribe to misguided prudery which depicts ordinary people's ordinary sex lives as too debased and animal to be referred to in public. We don't mind insidious sex, the kind that pretends it isn't sex at all. We're unruffled by sex masquerading as art, business or entertainment. We can even stomach articles on sexual technique, provided they're written by an expert, preferably with the title Dr. So ingrained is this hypocrisy that if you try talking about sex without disguising it as something else, people question your sanity/morality. Boobs and bums may be the public domain, but referring to whether or not most people actually enjoy sex emphatically isn't. Why not? 'Because', as I've been told over and over again, 'you just don't talk about things like that.' 'Why not?' 'Some things are private.'

Rubbish. Sex is part and parcel of every aspect of public life. You can't sell a packet of crisps without it. The only private thing about sex in 1994 is people's private, secret, unvoiced fears of inadequacy. Strictly private, forever under wraps are people's anxieties that their sex lives are somehow not normal. Routine treatment of sex in the media implies that perfect couples with perfect bodies indulge in total body and mind immersion while eating ice-cream. The sad truth is that reasonable, rational people everywhere torture themselves with their failure to measure up to this cruelly unattainable norm.

I thought we needed some honest answers to some unspoken questions. How many times a week is everyone else making love? Is it unnatural to loathe the taste of sperm? Is it peculiar to break wind during intercourse? Help! Where's my G-spot? So I've tried to answer them. What are my qualifications? I haven't any – except nine years in bed with the same husband. I've told it the way I see it. I hope the way I see it makes you feel better about the way you see it. And I wish you health, wealth and years of very merry fun-filled nights, toasting me in Ovaltine.